To Vanessa —
Thanks for being one of
my best ever clients.

C x

November 2020.

Regeneration Manchester
30 years of storytelling
Len Grant

Copyright © Len Grant 2020

The right of Len Grant to be identified as the author of this work has been asserted by him in accordance with the Copyright, Designs and Patents Act 1988.

Published by Manchester University Press
Altrincham Street, Manchester M1 7JA

www.manchesteruniversitypress.co.uk

British Library Cataloguing-in-Publication Data

A catalogue record for this book is available from the British Library

ISBN 978 1 5261 5798 0 hardback

First published 2020

The publisher has no responsibility for the persistence or accuracy of URLs for any external or third-party internet websites referred to in this book, and does not guarantee that any content on such websites is, or will remain, accurate or appropriate.

Design: Axis Graphic Design
Print: Graphius, Belgium

All images © Len Grant, except

p.38 Lauren Hyde

p.132, p.141 (bottom), p.162 David Oates

p.146 Sketches by Mike Hitchmough, © 3DReid

p.155 English Heritage listed building description by permission www.english-heritage.org.uk/list

p.157 (bottom) Courtesy Trafford Local Studies Centre

pp.168-173 Alan Ward

End papers: (front) The Bridgewater Hall; (rear) 1 Angel Square

For this volume, thanks to Rebecca Grant for proofreading and to friend and collaborator, Alan Ward who, for over 15 years, has enhanced my work with his thoughtful and meticulous design.

www.lengrant.co.uk

Regeneration Manchester
30 years of storytelling

Len Grant

Manchester University Press

Contents

April 2008: Photographed in Miles Platting by Jan Chlebik for TEN, an inward investment magazine for Manchester.

November 1990: Tony Wilson outside Factory Records' new headquarters on Charles Street.

June 1987: The Nottingham and Beeston Canal was the subject of my first picture story.

Tram tracks are being laid for the Metrolink to Altrincham and Bury. The tracks run across a new bridge alongside G-Mex before sweeping to street level close to Tommy Ducks, then on past the Dutch Pancake House, in front of the City Art Gallery and between Lewis's and the sunken Piccadilly Gardens.

Already the challenge of pulling our city out of its post-industrial malaise has begun. A new home for the Hallé orchestra is in the offing, and our magnificent redbrick Victorian warehouses are being converted to loft apartments, although we still call them flats. The pragmatic Labour-controlled council is partnering with a Tory government-imposed quango to improve the south and east of the city centre; and Manchester is punching above its weight to bid for the 1996 Summer Olympics. We don't stand any chance, but it demonstrates a civic optimism we hope will eventually pay off.

* * * *

There wasn't much to do in Manchester back then. If I had mates up for the weekend we'd have a day out in Liverpool. We'd do the cathedrals, the Tate, the ferry across the Mersey.

In Manchester, an evening out might include the Britons or the 'Pev', often both. A late meal involved the 42 bus over to Rusholme for seekh kebab and rogan josh; I don't recall ever eating in town.

Affleck's Palace would be incorporated into a weekend shopping trip, more out of curiosity than as a punter. I'd have to go on a Saturday because on Sundays everywhere was closed. Actually, town was dead for much of the week. Apart from the incoming loft-dwellers, the only city centre residents lived, bizarrely, in an enclave on the roof of the Arndale.

As a curious photographer with an expensive camera, I'd explore the quiet canal towpaths with one eye over my shoulder. Although places like Ancoats and Hulme were not exactly no-go areas, you did well to proceed with caution.

A century and a half earlier, the city was renowned worldwide for its export of cotton goods.

Manchester 1990

In 1990, it was football and music, neither of which I had much interest in.

United – and it was the Reds who had the international reputation – apparently surprised everyone, including themselves, by winning the FA Cup. The following season it was the European Cup Winners' Cup, but it'd be another nine years before they would parade a trio of trophies on an open-topped bus.

In May, The Stone Roses played their now legendary gig at Spike Island in Widnes. It passed me by, as did much of the Madchester scene, notwithstanding two or three nights at the Haçienda with more enlightened friends. Only now do I own a bucket hat.

As an emerging photographer in the city that spawned Factory Records I was more than aware of the prodigious output of music photographers Pete Walsh, Ian Tilton and Kevin Cummins and would look forward to each City Life issue – then an independent title – that regularly commissioned their work. My own contribution to the genre was a session at Salford Docks with indie band Man from Delmonte who I met while photographing artists in the city. I did, early on, grab a snap of Tony Wilson. Until now, it has never been published.

Having no TV, I followed the Strangeways riots – the worst in UK history – on the radio. Earlier that year, I'd listened to the news that Nelson Mandela had been released, and some months later, the welcome demise of Margaret Thatcher as Prime Minister. 1990 was also the year in which Tim Berners-Lee proposed a World Wide Web to share documents between computers, an idea that was to change all our lives.

* * * *

I became a photographer in 1990 almost by default. A decade earlier I'd attended Trent Polytechnic (now Nottingham Trent University) to do Business Studies. By all accounts the college ran a good BA Photography course at the time, to which I was oblivious. After four years I graduated and became a medical representative, promoting anti-inflammatory drugs to GPs in the East Midlands. Bored of doctors' waiting rooms, I then progressed to selling TV advertising airtime for Central TV, at first from their Nottingham office and then back in Manchester from 1987, based in their tiny satellite office behind Central Library.

In my sales executive days, photography was very much a hobby. While in Nottingham I signed up to an inspirational evening class, run by an enthusiastic commercial photographer. He taught me the significance of making a series of images to tell a story rather than, like many hobbyists, just seeking out that one 'killer' shot that might look good in a frame. For my first ever photo story, I took my Ricoh KR-10 SLR camera and documented the local canal, contrasting it with the parallel, busy boulevard. It was a start.

My weekends were spent in the darkrooms of an arts centre in Nottingham's Lace Market. It was Paul Wombell – years later to become director of The Photographer's Gallery in London – who asked me on my first visit if I'd used a darkroom before. I lied, but had a 'How to...' book in my bag and spent the next four hours making two prints.

Once in Manchester I joined Counter Image, a North West Arts Board-funded film, video and photography workshop based on Whitworth Street West, along from the Haçienda. Having been floundering on my own until now, it was a real boost to meet other photographers and filmmakers, attend workshops and be part of group exhibitions.

In 1988, I staged my first ever solo exhibition, Dead Arty, at Counter Image (see page 10). One fellow workshop member, a graduate from the much-revered photography degree down the road at Manchester Polytechnic, commented that my show was on a par with any university final show. That single comment boosted my confidence and, for a short time at least, neutralised the imposter syndrome that took root in those early days and has stayed with me ever since.

The TV sales job had by now given way to an equally unrewarding role as a new business executive for a small advertising agency in Wilmslow. On New Year's Day 1990 – the year I'd turn 30 – I pledged to start my freelance career on 1st June. I had no commitments, a bit of savings. If it all went wrong, I could go back to being a bad salesman.

So the career switch was motivated more by finding an escape route out of dull jobs than a huge desire to take photographs full time. But there was

August 1988: While still an amateur I shot some publicity stills for indie band Man from Delmonte.

March 1985: The first black and white film I processed included this portrait of my friend Janet at the back door of the house we shared in Nottingham.

another incentive too. In 1982, at the end of my college course, I'd suffered what was professionally described as a mild nervous breakdown. My twenties were subsequently overshadowed by anxiety and bouts of depression, by varying levels of medication and by trips to psychologists and the occasional psychiatrist. So, a career change at 30 was a fresh start. If I could make a success of self-employment, it might mean that I had at least tamed my demons, if not banished them completely.

In the months before my self-imposed start date, I bought myself a professional camera (a Bronica ETRS), went on more workshops, and sought advice wherever I could. I bought an Amstrad computer, a dot-matrix printer, a fax machine and one of those answer-machines you could call to pick up messages. I had my first business card and letterhead printed.

In retrospect my first commissions were nothing special: I photographed recently-installed conservatories for a Wirral double glazing company; huge shipping containers in Reddish; and a studio full of packaging products. But I loved it. I loved the freedom – and responsibility – of being my own boss, and I couldn't get over the concept of making a living (barely, at first) from being creative.

* * * *

Over 30 years, I've produced more than 25 books and held numerous exhibitions. Editing that creative output to fit these 176 pages has been a significant challenge. I began by considering my target audience. Is this book for proud Mancs who'd like to see before and after pictures of how their city has developed? Is it for the many regeneration professionals who, quite rightly, celebrate the city's success, and their part in it? Or, maybe, it's something fellow creatives can identify with, perhaps be inspired by?

Of course, it should be all of these, but in the end, it's none of them. Regeneration Manchester is my story. My story of each of the more significant projects; my story of the changes I've made to a storytelling process; my story of the failures as well as the successes.

With some commissions lasting years and generating hundreds of rolls of film or thousands of digital images, the edit is merely a skim over the surface. Many of the projects have their own standalone book (see pp.168-173), and there are

other images online, for those whose curiosities are piqued.

This book, then, is about the whole, and it's about the process. I now appreciate it's the day-to-day process of any one project that should be enjoyed and celebrated as much as the final product – the means and not just the ends. That's not to diminish the excitement I feel when I see strangers enjoying my work in an exhibition or when I smell a new book, fresh off the presses.

I've been fortunate. My photographic career has coincided with a remarkable period in our city's history. It's been a privilege to have played some part in recording that and I'm delighted to present a selection in Regeneration Manchester.

Len Grant
October 2020

To capture the best of the Manchester light, their studios were often on the top floors of dilapidated warehouses and mills dotted around the city centre.

And whilst still working as TV sales executive, I spent weekends and evenings setting up my 35mm Ricoh SLR – loaded with HP5 black and white film – in front of the city's artists. I called my project 'Dead Arty' and it was my first solo photography exhibition. I was delighted.

My endeavours came to the attention of a TV director, Phil Griffin, who was planning to make a documentary about the same subject. Phil introduced me to a commercial photographer, Mike Black, who, unknown to me, was also photographing the city's artists but in colour and on large format cameras.

During one week in September 1988 Mike and I toured the city's studios again, this time with a Granada TV crew in tow, as we photographed yet more artists for a half-hour documentary. 'The Art Mob' was screened the following January.

It was talking to Mike about his experiences that got me thinking of photography as a way out of my uninspiring sales career. Eighteen months later, I set up as a freelance photographer.

PROJECT:

Dead Arty, Photographs of Painters and Sculptors in Manchester 1988

Exhibited at Counter Image,
Manchester
October-December 1988

Artists, clockwise from
opposite, top:
Shirley Diamond,
Fiona Moate,
Ian Rawlinson,
Linda Weir,
Alan Buckingham.

Dead Arty

From *The Advertiser*, 25th July 1991:

'A new exhibition aimed at putting city folks in the picture will form an historic record of Salford.

For freelance photographer Len Grant has just been commissioned by the council's Viewpoint Gallery to record and capture the developing Salford of the 90s.

In the exhibition, called 'The New Era', Len will be looking at every aspect of present day life which highlights the rapid cultural, social and structural changes taking place.'

I had already started my City Shapers series – portraits of Manchester and Salford's movers and shakers (p.18) – when I applied for the commission from Salford City Council.

I was able to include images of Ted Hagan – the first developer to dip his toe into Salford Quays – and Manchester Council's Chief Planning Officer, Ted Kitchen, to demonstrate my 'people approach' to documenting change.

It worked. I spent the summer of 1991 working on an exhibition for the prestigious Viewpoint Gallery, just a year after becoming a freelance photographer.

COMMISSION:

Faces of Change: Salford's New Era 1991

Commissioned by Salford City Council

Exhibited at Viewpoint Gallery, Salford, October–December 1991

The exhibition included this image of Hilda White, chair of Thorn Court Residents' Association, who successfully campaigned for additional security measures and other improvements to her Pendleton high-rise block.

I photographed small businesses, an arts cooperative, and the residents of the housing scheme adjacent to Salford Lads' Club. While in a boat documenting young canoeists, I took a shot of local lads making their own entertainment at Salford Quays (following spread).

Over 30 black and white portraits were made altogether – local politicians, council officers, architects and planners amongst them – but the curator thought the exhibition needed some colour to reflect the city's renewed optimism. So, in collaboration with gallery staff, I made montages with painted backgrounds to accompany each image.

I loved Hilda White, perched on the claw of her settee in a room clad with horse brasses. Her friends, Flo, Queenie and Harriet, all in slippers and identical bi-focals, watch the budgie balancing on our Hilda's head. I was privy to see the contact strips of her juggling with cup and budgie: they seemed spontaneous and tactile, a rare find in this show.

Sue Platt, *City Life* review

As part of the commission brief I was required to keep a written record of my exploits.

<u>11th July 1991</u>: 'Yesterday I went to Chimney Pot Community Centre to meet community worker Bert Watson, a very interesting man. He's always lived in Salford and remembers, as a kid, having to go to Buile Hill Park if he wanted to see grass. The 'parkie' wouldn't let you walk on it though. He used to work on Salford Docks and reckons containerisation was the death of the docks. "Why sail eight hours to the Ship Canal when you can unload your cargo on the south coast and take it the rest of the way by road?"

'He told me of a tea dance he is helping to organise this afternoon... [later]... the lighting was really crap, coloured spotlights everywhere. We moved one of the tables into the middle of the room so it would be underneath a decent light. He was a good sitter but he did tend to freeze a little when I was taking shots.

'On the technical side I was using TMAX 400 rated at 800 because the light was so rubbish and even then only got about 1/60 at 5.6.'

Joe Valenta told me he'd paid 50p for a pensioner's day pass from the local angling club. Although the old docks had been cleaned up and stocked with fish, he'd had no success.

Angela Miller, front, and Lynn Gregson: local residents who got jobs at the newly-opened Sainsbury's supermarket on Regent Road.

The exhibition had an unexpected consequence. A year later I found myself on the steps of the National Portrait Gallery being introduced to one of my all-time heros, Jane Bown. Jane had worked for *The Observer* since 1949 and was well respected for her black and white portraits of celebrities.

I had been nominated for the Fox Talbot Prize at the 1992 ICI Photography Awards and was now mingling at an exhibition launch with the likes of Paul Reas, Tom Wood, Anna Fox, Steve Pyke and John Blakemore, that year's winner. I had all their books on my shelves.

As an 'emerging photographer' my inclusion in such a distinguished line-up was very much accidental. The nominees were selected by influential photographers, gallery directors and picture editors. Viewpoint was an important regional gallery but its new curator was, bizarrely, from a PR background and had no insight into contemporary photography. So my nominator was her boss, arts officer Graham Marsden, who had clearly been impressed with my recent exhibition.

To his credit, Graham's statement for the exhibition catalogue encapsulated an approach that would last my entire creative career:

'Len Grant's pictures are founded on a simple premise, all too often missing in contemporary documentary photography: he has a positive liking of people and a genuine interest in their lives. A strong urge to find out more, and a desire to pass on that information, makes for photographs which are accessible to as wide an audience as possible.'

16th August 1991: 'On Monday I will be photographing Roger Rees, the Chief Executive of the Council. I'm looking forward to it. I'm told his room is quite a den of newspapers, books and papers. Good, it sounds quite photogenic.'

Faces of Change

My timing was fortunate. I became a photographer just as the city's regeneration was gaining momentum. In 1991, as I embarked on a personal project to photograph the 'movers and shakers', several keys projects had just begun. The Central Manchester Development Corporation (CMDC) – a government quango – was investing in the south and east of the city centre and putting its weight behind the dream for a new international concert hall; Hulme had just won its City Challenge funding; Salford Docks became Salford Quays; and the city was bidding to host the 1996 Summer Olympics.

Some later commented I was shrewd to get myself in front of so many potential clients with this, a non-commissioned project. I didn't see it like that at the time; it was rather an opportunity to combine my interests in photographic portraiture and regeneration. In retrospect, many of the connections made were indeed fruitful.

As with all projects since, I struggled with the creative direction of 'Shapers'. This from my notebook, 19th April 1991: 'Getting very frustrated with what I'm doing. What will people think? What does it matter? Does anyone give a damn?

'I'm looking at my pictures and trying to imagine what other people (particularly those in photography) will think of them. Is there any depth? What sort of representation am I trying to achieve?

'I've come to a conclusion: I'm getting too close, step back. Take the pictures *you* want to take, for your own reasons.'

PROJECT:

City Shapers
1991-92

Exhibited at
The Charterhouse Hotel as part of the Boddingtons Manchester Festival, September 1992 and then toured the city

Ian Simpson
Simpson Associates

I included architect Ian Simpson in my City Shapers show because of his involvement with the Knott Mill Association. His exhibition caption read: 'Simpson and other design-related colleagues have already refurbished their own building, Commercial Wharf, and, with the help of Central Manchester Development Corporation, intend to gradually turn the whole area into commercial, leisure and residential space.' Indeed, Ian and others drew up a masterplan for Knott Mill in 1992.

Since then, Ian, with co-founding partner Rachel Haugh, have made a significant impact on the city's high-rise architectural landscape notably with Urbis, No. 1 Deansgate and Beetham Tower. The practice also assembled and led the team that won the city centre masterplanning competition following the 1996 IRA bomb.

SimpsonHaugh, as the practice is now known, is still very much behind the Knott Mill Association which, in 2019, submitted an updated masterplan for future development.

For three months after its launch, City Shapers toured to the Royal Exchange Theatre, the NatWest Bank on King Street, the Arndale Centre, the Town Hall and Central Library. Later it was shown at the British Council.

Ian Simpson

Dr Ted Kitchen

Dr Ted Kitchen

City Planning Officer, Manchester City Council

From my notebook, 9th April 1991: 'This morning I photographed Ted Kitchen – first session of the project. Was I nervous or what? Didn't sleep much last night. Was in his office at the Town Hall by 8.30 and didn't leave until 10...'

City Shapers

David Plowright
Chairman, Olympic Stadium Steering Committee

My exhibition caption read: 'As a former Mancunian of the Year it was to be expected that David Plowright's involvement in the city would not end after his pioneering chairmanship of Granada Television.

'During his time at Britain's oldest independent television company Granada used their expertise in entertainment to develop the most successful tourist attraction in Manchester, Granada Studios Tour.

'Opposite, the renovation of a waterside warehouse into a hotel marks the beginning of an equally ambitious project: Media City. Dubbed as 'Hollywood on the Irwell' it is planned as a mix of commercial and leisure facilities.'

Howard Bernstein
Deputy Chief Executive, Manchester City Council

Each time I photographed a subject for City Shapers, I asked them who else I should include. Howard Bernstein's name came up again and again.

In 1996 he became Chief Executive of the public-private partnership, Manchester Millennium, that coordinated the rebuilding after the IRA bomb. Two years later he took on the same role at the Council. He was knighted in 2003 following the successful Commonwealth Games the previous year. In 2017 he retired from the Council, which he had originally joined as a junior clerk.

Ted Hagan
Chairman and Managing Director, Urban Waterside Ltd

In the early 80s Salford City Council had bought acres of Salford Docks from Manchester Ship Canal Company and had commissioned architects Shepheard Epstein Hunter to develop a masterplan. The first developer on the newly-named Salford Quays was Urban Waterside.

From my notebook: 'Ted is quite shy and very difficult to pose, although he is not at all unwilling. The conditions weren't brilliant today... bright sunshine was intermittent and the wind was strong and cold. Ted's a nice bloke, never seems to be able to put into words what he wants to, and you can tell it infuriates him.'

David Plowright

Howard Bernstein > **Ted Hagan**

21   City Shapers

Lyn Fenton

Jim Ramsbottom

Bookie-turned property developer, Jim Ramsbottom had already had success with his Mark Addy pub before turning to Castlefield. As part of its remit, CMDC had the job of improving the canal-side infrastructure and Jim saw an opportunity. By the time I took this photo in his Dukes '92 pub, days before its opening in January 1992, he had already renovated the Lock-keeper's Cottage opposite and was converting nearby Gail House into Eastgate.

Before the potential of the creative industries was fully recognised, Jim very much considered the 'arty-farty crowd' as his target market.

Cllr Graham Stringer

Cllr Graham Stringer
Leader, Manchester City Council

Leader of the Labour-controlled Council since 1984 – it would be another five years before he was succeeded by Richard Leese – Graham Stringer was always uncomfortable in front of the camera. Perhaps this is why I chose to photograph him, apparently candidly, in the council chamber.

Lyn Fenton
Regional Manager, AMEC Regeneration

I photographed Lyn outside the gates of Manchester Cathedral as she was looking at the potential of the 'Northern Gateway' – an area including Victoria and Exchange Stations, Chetham's and the Cathedral. We worked together later when she headed Ancoats Urban Village Company and was involved in the early days of New Islington.

City Shapers also included: James Grigor (Chairman) and John Glester (Chief Executive) of Central Manchester Development Corporation; Peter Hadfield (Chairman) and Mike Shields (Chief Executive), Trafford Park Development Corporation; Bob Scott, Chairman of Manchester Olympic Bid Committee; Roger Stephenson, Stephenson Architecture; Robert Hough, Chairman, Manchester Ship Canal Company; Robert Taylor, Director General, British Council; Tony Struthers, Deputy Chief Executive, Salford City Council;

Andrew Ogg, Leslie Jones Architects; Herman Jungmayr; Martin Willey, Beaver Projects; Patrick Green, Director, Museum of Science and Industry; Mel Taylor, Hidden Hotels; Cllr Jack Flanagan, Chairman, Metrolink; Anton Rodgers, Architects Group Practice; David Barnes, BDP; Morenga Bambatta, Director, Nia Centre; Nick Whipp, Grimley JR Eve; Elizabeth Jeffries, Director, Greater Manchester Visitor Convention Bureau; Ray Birch, Commercial Manager, Wimpey Homes.

Lesley Whitehouse

Lesley Whitehouse
Chief Executive, Hulme Regeneration Ltd

The exhibition caption read: 'It could be said that Lesley Whitehouse has the most challenging job associated with Manchester's redevelopment.

'She is head of Hulme Regeneration, a non-profit making, joint venture company charged with rebuilding Hulme. Her five-year job, she says, is much more than housing (2,000 new homes will be built, half of them private). It is to do with the quality of people's lives. More jobs, better-quality jobs, a greener environment, a more 'normal-looking area'...'

The City Challenge programme – a Conservative government initiative introduced after inner city riots of the 80s – invited councils to select a neighbourhood and bid for a share of a pot of money. Each council was required to collaborate with residents on their bids and I was commissioned by Salford City Council to photograph brainstorming sessions as Pendleton residents got excited about what might be achieved on their inner city estate.

But City Challenge was a competition and in 1992 Manchester won and Salford lost. The divisive process left the residents of Pendleton, and many other areas around the country, feeling let down and forgotten. Pendleton had to wait many more years before cash came its way.

Over the border Hulme was celebrating. It was awarded a budget of £37million over five years and the public-private joint venture, Hulme Regeneration Ltd, was set up to spend it. Some objectives – like job opportunities and boosting the local economy – were influenced by external factors but the agency had greater control over providing more housing stock and improving the feel of the place.

This was Hulme's second revival in a generation. In the late 60s the last swathes of terraced houses were swept away in 'the clearances' to be replaced, in part, by four seven-storey crescent-shaped blocks inspired by Georgian Bath and London's Bloomsbury. This new, deck-access housing used factory-built concrete blocks that could be

assembled quickly on site. Within months of their completion in 1971, the Crescents were beset with defects – flooding, vermin and poor insulation. The so-called streets in the sky soon became stinking rat-runs for criminal behaviour.

Declared unfit for purpose, the Council abandoned the Crescents in 1984 and, until their demolition a decade later, they became squats and a hotbed for alternative creativity.

In many ways, the latest regeneration of Hulme broke new ground. It was the first time most Council officers had been involved in a whole neighbourhood-wide renewal programme that not only had to tackle physical housing, economic and social issues, but also required the collaboration of local people. Many of those officers took what they had learnt in Hulme in the mid 90s to new positions in east Manchester a few years later.

Cycling through Hulme's neighbourhoods as I occasionally do – checking out the houses, parks, and new roads that I photographed being built nearly 30 years ago – it's clear Hulme's second regeneration effort is outlasting its first.

One morning in October 1993 I joined the royal paparazzi pack – everyone but me had a step ladder – to snap Diana, Princess of Wales unveil the first homes to be completed in the new Hulme. There's still a plaque on the side of the house to mark the spot.

I recall the regeneration team failing to interest either of the universities, despite their proximity, in developing sites in Hulme in the early 90s. This is Bonsall Street (top left, 1997; top right 1995), now the site of Manchester Metropolitan University's Brooks Building and student accommodation blocks.

The Crescents were, ironically, named after prominent architects. This is John Nash Crescent (left) and Hawksmoor (right) being demolished in April 1994.

Above: the depressing Moss Side Shopping Centre and, with a controlled explosion, a high-rise housing block, are swept away in 1994, together with some industrial units to make way for Hulme High Street. By May 1995, Moss Side Leisure Centre stands alone on the cleared site.

Deputy Prime Minister, Michael Hesletine MP, architect of the City Challenge programme, poses alongside AMEC's Sir Alan Cockshaw for the Hulme High Street start on site photo opportunity, February 1997.

A new market, supermarket, shopping street and housing followed, notably the Buttress-designed Life Buildings that now anchor one end of the new street.

Most of my photography in Hulme was for promotional purposes. My images were used in press releases, slide presentations, brochures, and to illustrate the 15 issues of Hulme News, a community newsletter for which I also wrote some of the short articles.

My images very much reflected the 'official' image of the new Hulme – positive and upbeat – although I was aware of other photographers documenting a more accurate record of a community in flux.

This second regeneration of Hulme has generally been lauded a success: the population has increased significantly with improved quality and choice of housing. It has thrown off its reputation for crime and anti-social behaviour but has clung onto its bohemian character. It's now a very pleasant part of town.

The joint venture element of the programme gave the Council experience of working closely with the commercial sector (and, presumably, vice versa) which gave it a head start when, in 1996, it had to quickly build a broad public-private partnership to tackle the rebuilding following the IRA bomb.

My commission to document the building of the 19,000-seater indoor arena adjacent to Manchester's Victoria Station was the first of my construction projects. The contractors began by demolishing the cast iron canopies that spanned the outlying platforms. For a week over Christmas 1992, the trains were stopped as the roof came off. Remarkably, the rest of the construction programme was undertaken above live train lines.

For the second time Manchester was bidding to host the Summer Olympic Games with the arena earmarked as the venue for the basketball. Periodically during construction, groups of International Olympic Committee members would tour the site. In September 1993, an expectant crowd filled Albert Square to hear Manchester come third behind Beijing and Sydney, the eventual host. The bid was not futile – we had beaten Berlin and Istanbul after all – and our communal morale was boosted. In 2002 Manchester would stage the XVII Commonwealth Games, brilliantly.

Arena! was my first book and my aspiration was to make a publication in the style of the photobooks that inspired me. I commissioned documentary photographer Anna Fox to help me sequence the images and Deyan Sudjic, architecture critic for *The Guardian,* to write an introduction.

Once published, the book was parodied by some in the project team, replacing my captions with their own, to produce a tongue-in-cheek version.

COMMISSION:

Arena
1992-95

Commissioned by
Vector Investments

Published as Arena! in 1995
by Len Grant Photography

Christmas Eve 1992: This was my first visit to the station. The *Evening News* had reported that this would be the last day these platforms would be operating before demolition began. It soon became obvious that not everyone was here to catch a train.

An old man was walking the length of each platform. Back and forth, then down through the tunnel and up onto the next. "A real shame," he said when he saw me with the camera. "Why couldn't they have just refurbished it?"

I told him I was doing a documentary project for the developers. "So you're the culprits, then?" he said. I hadn't thought of it like that.

On platform 12 two men were photographing each other against the cast iron canopy. "My dad used to bring me down here to watch the trains come through," one told me. "The steam would go right up into the roof there." He pointed to a corner of the derelict canopy, from where a pigeon flew out.

I could see these two from the other side of the site.

They were collecting bits of twisted metal from what remained of the Red Star offices. Amongst the excavators and the cranes they were far from inconspicuous, but the workers were happy enough to ignore their pilfering. One less job, no doubt.

I started towards them but they saw me approaching and were quickly over the rubble and out the gate. I followed across the road and around the corner of the furniture store, calling after them.

The elder boy, seeing I had nearly caught up with his younger brother, took a piece of piping out of his cart and came back to challenge me.

"I only want to take your photo," I started to explain. They both looked at me in disbelief.

"A quid," the eldest replied eventually.

"What?"

"A quid to take a picture. Each."

It wasn't exactly the kind of documentary shot I'd had in mind.

"I tell my wife that we're never more than ten feet off the ground in this job. She'd die if she knew what we get up to."

'Topping out' celebration, 23rd November 1994, with singer Mick Hucknall
and celebrity steeplejack, Fred Dibnah.

You'd have to be blind not to notice the changes in the Manchester landscape over the last five years. After spending much of the 80s attempting to cling to its industrial past, the 90s has seen the city's fathers gripped by a new realism, finally realising that these days – whether you like it or not – the prosperity of the city is intrinsically linked to its leisure time activities (see Manchester United and the city's thriving nightlife/music culture for the most obvious proof).

Hence the construction of the NYNEX Arena, on the site of the old platforms of Victoria Station, which this book documents through words and pictures, but mostly through the latter. Manchester photographer Len Grant has done a marvellous job here, beginning with shots of those soon to be demolished platforms and the people working there, before embarking on a blow by blow account of the building process.

The sheer scale of the Arena and the resources it has taken to build it, is one impressive aspect to the story being told here, but that's not all. In the same way that it is impossible to get a real sense of the building without the spectators it was built for (the recent Oasis gig really put the Arena's grand scale and post-industrial beauty into perspective for me), this book is not just about bricks and mortar, girders and concrete: it also gives a face and a voice to the people whose brains and brawn built it.

Chris Sharratt. *City Life* book review, 1995

"You're not from the paper, then?"

"No, it's for a book about the arena."

"You ought to do a book about Wet Wet Wet and then you'd sell loads."

Having photographed City Planning Officer Ted Kitchen as part of my City Shapers project, I approached him with a proposal to document the construction of the much-anticipated international concert hall, the city's first new civic building since King George V opened Central Library in 1934.

He liked the idea and approached funding partner, Central Manchester Development Corporation to share the cost. They were less keen, not on the idea of the documentation, but on commissioning one photographer over a period of several years.

Not content with their reply, Ted wrote back, 'What is really at stake here is not the issue of work for a particular photographer, but two very simple concepts.

'The first is that the new Concert Hall and associated developments will be the flagship project of the Development Corporation's lifespan, and therefore it deserves the best recording arrangements possible.

COMMISSION:

The Bridgewater Hall 1993-96

Commissioned by Manchester City Council

Published as Built to Music, The Making of The Bridgewater Hall, 1996

'The second is that we are remarkably careless with our contemporary history and, as a consequence, we constantly lose opportunities to record properly what we are doing now that is changing the face of the city; and once gone, these opportunities are gone forever.'

The Corporation relented and shared the cost. Ted later wrote to me: 'I think you know from our previous discussions how much importance I attach to this. I do think there is an unmissable opportunity here to record and then publish in appropriate forms the creation of a very significant piece of Manchester's contemporary history, and I am very excited by the prospect.'

Three years, and over 250 rolls of film later, the City Council published the 96-page book, Built to Music to mark the opening of The Bridgewater Hall.

March 1993: Once site of a dyeing and bleaching works and, up until the 70s, a bus station, Lower Mosley Street was about to be home to the city's new international concert hall.

"We're always knackered by the time we finish here. Up and down ladders all day, and all this fresh air. Last night I got in, had my tea, and then fell asleep in front of the telly from 8 o'clock until 10."

"I've been doing this since I left school. I'm 23 now and I'm still at home. I give 30 quid to my mam, and that's it. I'm loaded."

It's the norm now for a large construction project to be completed by a series of subcontractors, each taking on different stages of the process. I recall Laing North West being particularly proud to have their own team on site pretty much throughout the entire construction of The Bridgewater Hall. For me, it meant I got to know the same faces – the Valentine twins, for instance (bottom left) – and, while capturing the latest progress, I'd distribute photographs taken of the workers on my previous visits.

Looking south with The Britons Protection pub on the corner of Great Bridgewater Street, top right.

The stage area, in blue plastic, is taking shape and atop the visible foundation columns are green-cased isolation bearings. These effectively create a cushion on which the building sits, ensuring no ground vibration is felt – from a passing tram, for instance – inside the auditorium.

The Hall is so well isolated acoustically that, apparently, those rehearsing on stage on 15th June 1996 were totally oblivious to the explosion half a mile away.

As a self-taught photographer in the early 90s, my understanding of the world of professional photography came from books, magazines, the odd workshop and what I could glean from others. That knowledge had to be supplemented in the following years as the creative industries converted from analogue to digital – I started gradually and cautiously from about 2003.

During my film years my workhorse was the Bronica ETRS, a medium format camera that gives a larger negative than a regular 35mm camera. The interchangeable backs meant I could swap quickly between colour and black and white film, without having to finish the roll, and my rucksack would carry the spare back, film and different lenses.

My film choice was often quite crude: I'd shoot colour in bright conditions and black and white when it was dull. Or, I might choose monochrome to convey a particular mood, as with these steel fabricators. Once edited for publication or exhibition, my images were further enhanced with subtle split tones by photographic printer Marshall Walker, as with this shot of the upside down cantilever that supported the hall's immense roof.

A decision was made when we were compiling the book to have it ready for the opening of the Hall. With printing lead times, this meant I was taking images of the apparently completed building several weeks before it was actually finished. Even with careful composition, the occasional scaffold tower crept into my pictures as workers made finishing touches.

The published book, then, shows nothing of bustling foyers and excited concert-goers taking their seats which, in retrospect, was an omission. What is a concert hall without its audience?

In fact, I missed out on documenting the much anticipated opening night, my anxiety having got the better of me. My duties were delegated to my good friend, Jan Chlebik, who was further commissioned to document the completed – and occupied – Hall which he did brilliantly.

Five years later, for the book about The Lowry's construction, we delayed printing until we'd included several pages of celebrations as visitors teemed to Pier 8 for the opening weekend of Salford's new arts centre. It was a fitting ending.

Throughout the construction process my images were used in a regular newsletter and in a rolling exhibition in one of the windows of the Town Hall Extension. I worked with the Planning Department's graphic designer who – having requested prints of my images at exactly the size they'd be used – meticulously made up each display panel with galleys of type output from a phototypesetting machine and pasted into position alongside my images.

Of course, I gave special mention in the back of the book to Ted Kitchen, whose persistence had resulted in my commission. By the time of its publication, however, he had left the Council to become Professor of Planning and Urban Regeneration at Sheffield Hallam University.

Len puts the rebirth of a city into focus

■ A RIVETING STORY ... photographer Len Grant and one of his striking images documenting the building of the Bridgewater Hall, which is to be opened by the Queen tomorrow

By Janine Watson

PHOTOGRAPHER Len Grant is recording the changing face of Manchester.

He has just completed a photographic record of Manchester's most important new building — the stunning international music venue, the Bridgewater Hall.

He started to record the development as soon as the first digger went on site.

Len, who lives in Manchester, had started to record the changes in the inner city shortly after he became a photographer in 1990. He is currently documenting all the changes in Hulme.

Len, who has already produced a photographic book about the city's new Nynex Arena, said: "The regeneration of the city is fascinating.

"It is so sad that there are so few photographs of the construction of major buildings like the town hall.

"I'm not concentrating on architectural photographs but rather photographs that tell the story of how these developments were put together."

The Bridgewater Book — Built to Music — was commissioned by Manchester city council and Central Manchester Development Corporation.

The 90-page book covers the first excavators on site to completion of the £42m building.

It also describes the history of the site on Great Bridgewater Street.

Len is now hoping to become involved in recording the building of Salford's Lowry Centre.

He also wants to trace the development of the Manchester stadium. Dr James Grigor, chairman of CMDC and Coun Graham Stringer, former leader of the city council, said they commissioned Len to be on hand with his camera during the three-and-a-half years it took to build the hall.

"From the very first breaking of ground, he recorded the efforts of men and women who toiled on this landmark building," they said.

Those of us in Manchester on Saturday, 15th June 1996 will always remember what we were doing at 11.20am. My partner and I were in the garden of our Fallowfield semi with Rebecca, still a toddler.

Unlike the news photographers, I had no desire to rush into town with my camera and it was some days before I ventured to the cordon to see the devastation caused by a 3,300lb IRA bomb.

The City Council was quick off the mark and by 1st July had set up Manchester Millennium, a public-private partnership to coordinate the rebuilding of the city centre. Later that month a competition was launched to appoint a team of architects and urban planners to draw up a masterplan.

I was working on Hulme's regeneration at the time and was well placed to be commissioned to follow the work. But it would be another six months before I took my first photographs. Many of the bomb-damaged buildings were by then protected with plastic sheets. Others, like the Marks and Spencer store, were already being demolished.

After the Bomb
1997-99

Commissioned by
Manchester Millennium

Presented as a 96-metre hoarding along New Cathedral Street

Over the next two years I had unprecedented access to each of the demolition and then construction sites and amassed an archive of unique images. As with all my regeneration projects, each visit was different. An image captured on one day could not be replicated the next.

Partway through my documentation I was also commissioned by Richard Developments to follow, in greater detail, the transformation of Maxwell House – established as Withy Grove Printing House in 1873 – into The Printworks entertainment complex. The façade was retained and covered with a huge hoarding in the style of a newspaper, while everything behind it was demolished. A whole matrix of wonderfully photogenic steel grew behind the hoarding that would form the 'street' and cinemas. It was perhaps the last time I photographed steel erectors working directly on beams before safety regulations required them to use manriding baskets and cherry pickers.

Once the steel was complete and the roof on, I recall enjoying my visits far less. The site became a depressing warren, lit only by temporary, artificial light.

Marks and Spencer's: (left), the characteristic wavy canopy had already gone by February 1997 and, six months later, the demolition contractors were dismantling the basements (right). An online magazine later incorrectly attributed this demolition to the bomb explosion.

May 1997: Everything in this image between
the Corn Exchange (with exposed dome, left) to
the Royal Exchange (right), was subsequently
demolished. The timber-framed Sinclair's Oyster
Bar and adjoining Old Wellington Inn, snuggling in
the middle of the concrete Shambles Square, were
dismantled and moved (p.54). The road junction
became Exchange Square and the Arndale Centre
– which many had hoped might also be demolished
– was extended and re-modelled.

Maxwell House had been derelict for nearly a decade when Leo White and I signed in with the lone security guard and took a tour.

"I moved to the *Daily Mirror* as northern news editor in 1969 and this place was almost certainly Kemsley House back then," he says, as we go down into the basement. "Kemsley was the old newspaper dynasty, they owned the *Evening Chronicle*, the *Sunday Chronicle*, and the *Daily Dispatch*. They also had the *Sporting Chronicle*, and the *Formbook*.

"By the time I left it had become Thompson House and then Maxwell House. Whilst I was here newspaper production didn't change at all. We were always doing it the same way until the end, when Maxwell came.

"It was very posh down here: marble floors, mahogany-panelled walls, decorative glass doors almost from a different age. They had window screens to keep out the traffic noise. The parquet flooring was worth a fortune and beautiful at the time, obviously it's ruined now. It looks totally different stripped out. Quite sad.

"The press hall looks very different now because the floor above has been taken out. Back then it had a low ceiling with the presses in a long line along here.

"It was incredibly noisy and very busy. The whole building would shake once the presses started. We were three floors up on the editorial floor and you could even feel it there.

"Before my time pony and traps used to clatter down Balloon Yard to Victoria Station. You can imagine the horses coming along here and screeching to a halt. Newspaper drivers always thought they had to get from 0 to 60 in as many seconds as they had fingers. To this day, they still do.

"Here we are, home is where the heart is. This was the newsroom, our newsdesk was there. I'd sit here, my deputy opposite me. I'd have an assistant there and the Irish Editor and picture desk would be over there. The reporters' benches were all along the back.

"We'd watch that clock all day, especially if you were having a tough time. It used to tick, tick, and drop over. It was the focal point of the room really. I'd be watching from my desk, the reporters would be watching it, the chief sub, the night editor, everyone.

"In the newsroom we had guys who were called messengers but some of the older chaps used to shout 'boy!'. It wasn't derogatory, it was just something they'd always shouted. Then, in the rebellious mood of the early 70s, the messengers got a bit uppity and thought it was demeaning to be called messenger. So they were re-designated 'editorial assistants' which sounded better. If you felt inclined, you might then shout 'editorial assistant!' and they'd get very uptight about that.

"These posters tell you how many letters you can get to the inch, and how tall the letters will be. This is the number of the type. Instead of having to write 'tempo bold italic' you just put 583 x CAPS. It was a reference number really. We didn't use a lot of them."

The Maxwell House façade
was 'pinned' in place as
everything behind it was
demolished to make way for
The Printworks.

The eclectic mix of vintage paraphernalia traders that had stalls in the rundown Corn Exchange (above) never returned after the explosion. Instead owners Frogmore Investments saw an opportunity to refurbish the Grade II listed building into an ill-fated upmarket shopping centre that it unimaginatively branded 'The Triangle'.

Since then, and under different ownership, The Triangle has, thankfully, reverted back to being The Corn Exchange. I was back in the building in 2014 photographing the strip out of the retail units and the early stages of 5plus architects' sensitive conversion into a 'dining destination' and a 114-bedroom 'aparthotel'.

Just 50 metres away from the bomb blast, the Royal Exchange Theatre suffered significant structural damage. The theatre company decanted across town to the Upper Campfield Market on Liverpool Road where the show went on for the next two years.

With a £32m National Lottery grant the building was beautifully renovated and a 90-seater studio space added. It re-opened in November 1998.

After the Bomb

Left: This is one of my favourite images from the city centre rebuilding commission.

The 16th-Century Old Wellington Inn, and alongside it, Sinclair's Oyster Bar, sit amongst a landscape of concrete. In the foreground, the remains of Marks and Spencer, in the background the Market Place shopping area.

These two historic pubs had already been raised over a metre to fall into line with their 1970s neighbours, and now, as part of the post-bomb masterplan, they were moving again. This time, they'd be carefully dismantled and reassembled 300 metres away to a more appropriate setting adjacent to the Cathedral.

Architects from Buttress spent months on site overseeing the recording of every detail of both pubs' timber frame and roof construction so each could be reconstructed as accurately as possible.

It took two years for the pubs to be rebuilt – at right angles to each other this time – between The Mitre Hotel and The Corn Exchange. They pulled their first pints in September 1999 and have been a popular addition to the Medieval Quarter ever since.

After the Bomb

Working with Hemisphere Design, I exhibited my images of the city centre rebuilding along a 96-metre hoarding running the length of New Cathedral Street. The exhibition told the story of how the city had turned the dreadful event of 15th June 1996 into a opportunity to reinvent itself.

The enabling works – building a waterproof diaphragm along two sides of the triangular site – were already underway when The Lowry Trust launched a competition to choose a project photographer. I was one of two shortlisted after the first round of the competition. To help the panel make their decision, a photojournalist and I were both given a small fee, and a couple of months, to make work that demonstrated our approaches.

My emphasis was, of course, on people. Although the headline of my documentary work is the regeneration of the Manchester city region, the subtitle has always been, the people who have made it happen.

On the front page of my written submission I quoted the American curator, John Szarkowski:

'Architecture is not only a collection of buildings, it is a process... Photography of architecture should be less preoccupied with the finished building – an object – and more interested in the human and technical processes which proceed and produce it.'

So I set about getting myself in front of the relevant people so I might tell their stories.

COMMISSION:

The Lowry
1997-2000

Commissioned by
The Lowry Trust

Published as Making the Lowry in 2000 by the Lowry Press. Also exhibited as part of the opening exhibition programme

Architect Michael Wilford was an obvious choice. He and his partner, Sir James Stirling, had worked together for over 30 years, and it was their joint practice that had been shortlisted by the City Council to come up with a design for an arts centre on the end of a disused Salford dock.

As they were refining their ideas in June 1992, Stirling died following a routine operation. A month later – and what a month that must have been – Wilford presented to the Council and its partners and won the commission.

Stirling subsequently gave his name to the annual RIBA architectural prize, the equivalent of the Booker or the Turner Prize – a prize that Michael Wilford and Partners won in 1997 for The Music School in Stuttgart.

I spent a day at the practice's London studio photographing Wilford and his colleagues. I also photographed the staff at a local diner (to emphasise the economic impact The Lowry would have), and a biologist taking water samples from the docks (the environmental impact). These, and other portraits, highlighted my storytelling approach and I was subsequently taken on to capture not only the build but all the 'behind the scenes' activities.

The 176-page book, Making the Lowry was just one volume in the newly-created Lowry Press imprint. It was written by design journalist and academic Jeremy Myerson and designed by Hemisphere.

July 1997, left
September 1997, right.

The Lowry

Steel and skies: The study tower (above, July 1999) reaches its pinnacle; roof trusses are lifted above the 460-seater Quays Theatre (July 1998); and (opposite, April 1998), the partially-complete steel framework of the Lyric Theatre. Beyond, Huron Basin is, so far, undeveloped.

January 1999: Assembled in a nearby dry dock, the 96-metre Lowry footbridge was sailed into position on its second attempt, strong winds having thwarted engineers the previous day.

28th January 1999: 'Stephen Hetherington [Chief Executive] was a bit annoyed today. He'd previously had a meeting with Jeremy Myerson [book author] and changed the structure of the book but, it seems, the new direction has not found its way to me.

'Stephen wants more of a sense of achievement, of camaraderie, of…. he is so eloquent, he has lots of intangible requirements for the book but not a lot I could say was a brief. He wants me to interpret his vision but there's nothing to grasp hold of that I can actually turn into a strategy for working.

'What he does hark back to is people. And looking through my contact sheets I have precious few people, apart from PR shots and the yellow-vested site visits. These are so boring and I'm taking them for the record but I know they will never, ever be used. So where do I go from here? That is, after all, why I'm writing this. To write and to think.'

1st May 2000: 'Bank Holiday Monday. It's the third day of The Lowry opening weekend and I'm taking a day off. I'm exhausted. I've covered the run-up and the opening events, day and night. I need to spend some time with the children and to remember what little Daniel looks like [our third child was born two weeks earlier]. I've subcontracted work today to Jason [Lock] but I still feel as if I should be there, taking pictures.

'This weekend has been difficult. There has been too much stress and I can't help feeling I have only been through the motions and not taken any decent pictures. I still need a cover shot for the book. Somehow I am past caring, the book will be printed and published and, within weeks, forgotten about, as people move on to other things. My stress levels seem inappropriate for the final result.'

I was photographing the construction of Manchester Airport's second runway at the same time as I was documenting The Lowry at Salford Quays. The two projects couldn't have been more different.

The Lowry couldn't come soon enough. It was to be the catalyst for the regeneration of the redundant docks. It was to spearhead Salford's economic recovery.

Before the first bulldozer had set caterpillar tracks on the Bollin Valley, the second runway was already mired in controversy. The wider business case may have been sound but the environmental impact was immense. Despite promises to relocate endangered amphibians and colonies of bats, build new ponds and re-establish habitats, the project was targeted by environmental protestors.

My first roll of film for 'R2', then, was not of hi-vis-clad workers or huge earthmoving machinery, but of the makeshift camps the protestors had set up just off the A538.

As the Airport's 'official' runway photographer, I could have been seen as 'the enemy'. Instead I explained that my documentation should include, in my view at least, everyone's perspective, and I was left to photograph the camp and its occupants without any hassle.

It was rumoured that 'Swampy' – recently made famous as the last tunnelling protestor to be evicted from the A30 site in Devon – was also making tunnels here, and living in one of the rapidly-constructed treehouses, although I never saw him.

Within weeks the camps had been surrounded and an eviction by the Under-Sheriff of the County Sheriff's Office was underway. Now regarded as a member of the media, I was required to attend the Main Reception, Accreditation and Briefing Area before each of my visits. From here journalists, TV crews and 'snappers' were escorted to a Controlled Press Point – a pen in a field – from where we could see very little but awaited an occasional briefing from the Under-Sheriff.

Following a spirited stand from the 'trespassers', the area was eventually cleared and construction work started. For many months the site was characterised by mile upon mile of low plastic fencing which 'caught' frogs and newts before they could be re-housed elsewhere.

Manchester Airport's Second Runway 1997-2000

Commissioned by
Manchester Airport plc

I found working on the runway project difficult. Logistically it was hard. I'd have to drive to the works compound and wait for someone to give me a lift to the part of the massive site that I wanted to document. And wading through mud for much of the day was no fun.

Aesthetically it was unrewarding too. There was nothing for me to get my teeth into. Compared to The Lowry with its intriguing angles and shapes, the runway was one-dimensional. The only respite was the construction of a tunnel to allow the River Bollin to continue its course across the site. At last, something tall.

My client – the PR department at the Airport – commissioned a writer to provide the text for a proposed book that would celebrate the runway's completion. My designer friends at Hemisphere made a good job of putting it all together. The plan was for the book – The Long Haul – to be printed by August 2001. But there was a delay, maybe two, and the schedule got pushed back to October. Then 9/11 happened and everyone concerned with airports obviously had more pressing priorities.

My R2 pictures have never been published.

The Second Runway

The Second Runway

4th February 1999: 'The weather constantly annoys me.
Overcast and showery this morning as I was being ferried around
the runway site. Crap light, didn't even take my camera out of the
case. Now, cloudy but sunny with blue sky around and I'm waiting
to be taken to a hanger to photograph a mockup of an air traffic
control desk. Always the case: dull while I'm outside and sunny
while I'm inside. I take it out on myself, blame myself, create an
inner turmoil. It's crazy.'

The Second Runway

25th September 2000: 'Work more slowly. Use a tripod from time to time. Be prepared to wait for different elements in the picture to come together. Who are you doing it for? The client or yourself? Start to take more pictures you like rather than ones you think your client will like. Take three good pictures a day rather than six rolls of film. Keep training, continue to learn. Periodically examine your work practice. Why this film/camera/format? Why not another? Would it make the pictures different? Write more about what you are doing and why. Who is your target audience?'

I admit that, when I first started photographing in Ancoats, I'd hide my camera under my coat. The tall mills, narrow pavements and tiny streets that now give the first industrial suburb its heritage vibe felt decidedly unsafe 20 years ago.

At first mine was a 'watching brief', periodically walking the deserted streets to record the crumbling buildings or document small scale renovation. And then, from 2003, after wholesale compulsory purchase orders, the renovation of Ancoats' most iconic buildings got underway, notably Murrays' Mills, McConnel & Kennedy's Mills, St Peter's Church and Jactin House. I spent many hours in hard hat and hi-vis, photographing the beginning of what has to be one of the city's most successful turnarounds.

COMMISSION:

Ancoats
1999-2008

Commissioned by
Ancoats Urban Village
Company, and later by
New East Manchester Ltd

My dad's whole working life was in Manchester's declining textile industry. He told us he 'bought and sold yarn' and on our rare visits to the Royal Exchange Theatre he'd point out the brass plaques set in the parquet flooring that marked where the cotton traders once stood.

He'd also recall visits to his customers in Ancoats, small scale manufacturers, most likely the last occupants before the mills became derelict. Perhaps, in 2003, as I was photographing the rows of abandoned sewing machines or decaying patterns, I was literally following in my dad's footsteps.

It would be another 15 years before my daughter followed in my own footsteps when she spent some months as a tenant in one of the new apartments.

Left: McConnel and Kennedy's Mills, June 1999
Right: Murrays' Mills, April 2003

Ancoats

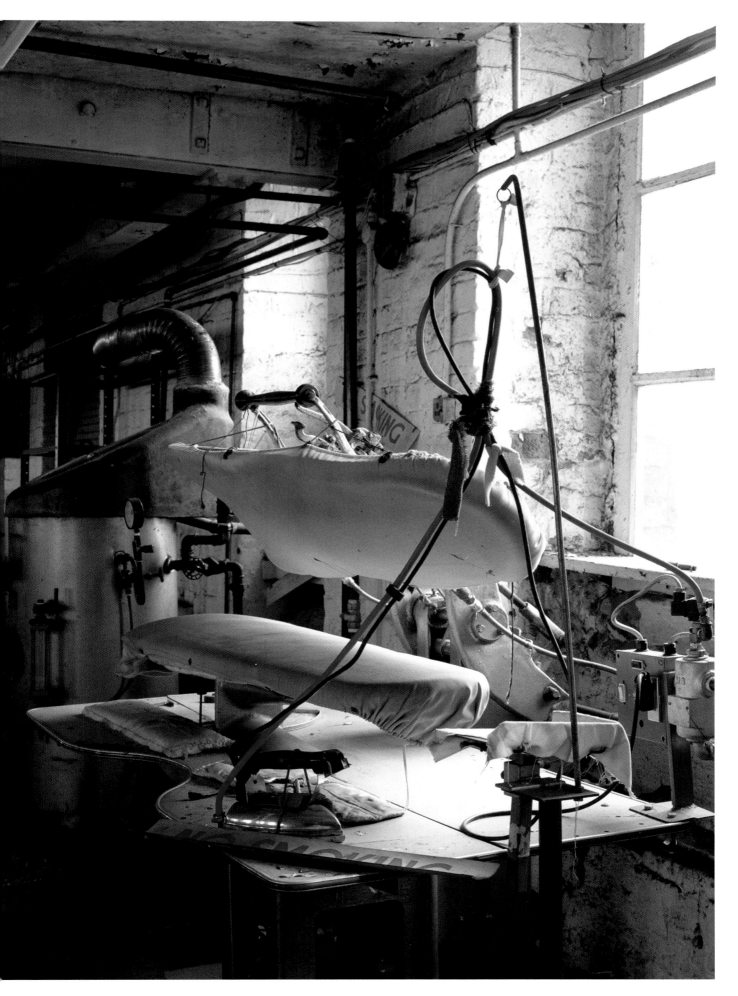

Murrays' Mills, April 2003: At the end of the eighteenth century, two Scottish brothers, Adam and George Murray, built a quadrangle of mills right besides the newly-opened Rochdale Canal. A canal basin inside their complex allowed for coal and raw cotton to be delivered direct, and for yarn to be dispatched.

From 2003, I photographed a programme of restorative work that effectively halted decades of decay.

Murrays' Mills then stayed empty until 2014 when Manchester Life Development Company took on this most important icon of the city's heritage and converted it into 124 apartments.

Architects Feilden Clegg Bradley Studios' sympathetic restoration has included adding a new block to replace one mill since detroyed, and so re-establish the inner courtyard in which landscape architects Planit IE acknowledge the original basin in their tranquil design.

McConnel and Kennedy's Mills (probably better known as their constituent parts: Royal, Sedgwick, Sedgwick New and Paragon Mills) were also developed by Scottish entrepreneurs in the 1790s.

I like the story of how John Kennedy was able to adapt Samual Crompton's spinning mule to run on steam power – and make vast profits – because Crompton had omitted to take out a patent on his original design.

In June 2003, when these pictures were taken, the dilapidation here was more advanced than at Murrays'.

With the help of a grant from the since defunct North West Development Agency, ING Real Estates, an arm of the Dutch banking giant, bought the crumbling mills in 2003. They were restored and converted into hundreds of apartments with an impressive glazed atrium between Royal and Sedgwick Mills.

McConnel & Kennedy's Mills,
October 2003–February 2005

The story of Ancoats, its history and subsequent renaissance, is well documented elsewhere. But much credit for this recent revival is due to the Ancoats Buildings Preservation Trust, a band of volunteers set up in 1995 to promote the area as an 'urban village'.

In an essay from 1996, one of those volunteers, architect Ian Finlay, co-wrote this vision: 'Ancoats 2020 is the classic urban village. All the important elements of the area's industrial past have been preserved and the area attracts a significant number of visitors. 'The Village' is vibrant, energetic and secure, playing a vital role in the international city of Manchester.

'New life has been breathed back into the area with the creation of a new resident community living in a mix of houses, sheltered accommodation and mills converted into flats, studio apartments and loft houses. A fine selection of housing is available for sale and rent...'

Jactin House: (below, October 2003; bottom, May 2005) was opened in 1891 as a shelter for homeless men.

The 2005 renovation of Grade II listed St Peter's Church (top, May 2005; above and right, April 2006) by Buttress, created a new rehearsal space for the Hallé orchestra.

The foreground of this right-hand image is now the popular Cutting Room Square.

Gorton Monastery – officially the Church and Friary of St. Francis – had been sold by the departing Franciscan brothers in the late 80s to a developer whose plan to turn the building into flats thankfully fell through. By the time a charitable trust had been established to save Edward Pugin's gothic masterpiece, much of it had been vandalised and its contents stolen.

In 2000 I was invited by the tenacious Elaine Griffiths, (she and her husband Paul founded the Trust) to take pictures of an open day (right), where visitors were given tours and invited to share their memories.

Over subsequent years I visited regularly, documenting a Christmas carol service here, a community dance event there. The Monastery is special to so many people – my own grandparents were married there – and the Trust and its team of volunteers has always put local people at the centre of its endeavours.

After a long-running fundraising campaign which eventually brought in over £6.5m, restoration finally got underway in 2005. Many of the stolen items had been tracked down, returned and re-installed.

Following its official re-opening in 2007, The Monastery Manchester – as it is now known – has continued its renovation and is now a successful weddings and events venue, the profits from which are channelled back into local charitable projects.

Gorton Monastery 2000-08

Latterly commissioned by New East Manchester Ltd

In 1998, the 5-metre stone crucifix – stolen from the church years earlier – was listed in a Sotheby's catalogue, about to be sold by an art dealer to a church in Florida. The Trust persuaded the dealer to keep the crucifix until it had raised enough funds for its return. In 2006, I photographed it being reinstalled above the high altar.

The twelve statues of 'The Saints' have a similar story. They were spotted by a local volunteer listed as 'garden ornaments' in a Sotheby's catalogue in 1994, each with a £2,000 reserve. The City Council intervened, bought them all, and had them brought back to Manchester. Restored onsite by volunteers, they were returned to their plinths in 2012.

When the construction budget was slashed from £40 million to £28 million – lottery funding was not forthcoming – architect Daniel Libeskind had to make some changes to his 'shattered globe' design. Instead of concrete each of the three 'shards' were made of steel which, for a photographer, were much more interesting. Nothing beats shooting shiny steel against a blue sky.

With every surface curved to mimic the curvature of the earth, it was a challenging structure to build but fascinating to photograph. The significance of documenting Libeskind's first building in the UK was not lost on me.

My images, of course, included the different trades from the piling contractors to the fit-out teams, and everyone in between. I was delighted to be reacquainted with those I'd photographed on previous jobs, including the Valentine twins, last seen on The Bridgewater Hall site (p.38).

COMMISSION:

Imperial War Museum North 2000-02

Commissioned by Imperial War Museum

Exhibited as Land Marks in the opening exhibition programme

5th January 2000: Ground-breaking with Daniel Libeskind, IWM trustee, Kate Adie and Culture Secretary, Chris Smith MP.

Imperial War Museum North

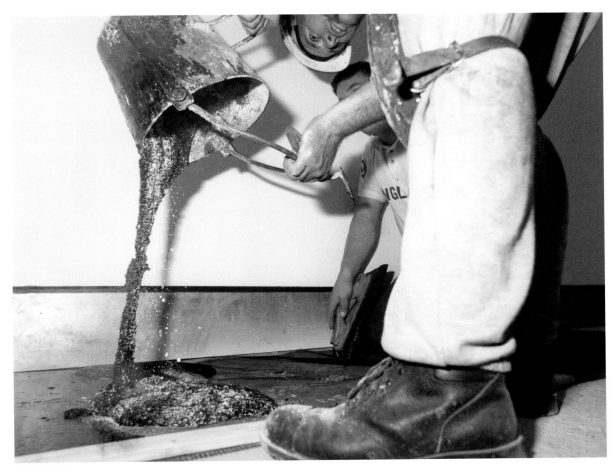

Imperial War Museum North

Working with curator Michael Simpson, I created Land Marks, which ran from July-November 2002 in the temporary exhibition gallery.

On one wall I exhibited 17 large black-and-white portraits of the workers, all shot on my vintage Mamiya twin lens reflex camera.

As part of this commission, I also experimented with sound for the first time, making hours of site recordings and interviewing workers, engineers, architects, and specialist sub-contractors. With Andrew Revell, we produced an emotive soundtrack that accompanied a synchronised slideshow of hundreds of my images projected onto the huge gallery walls.

Imperial War Museum North

'The special quality that Len Grant brings to his work is himself; his openness and his ability to put people at their ease. It is never a problem having Len around, which is why people open to him.'

Writer Phil Griffin's introduction to my mid-term retrospective in 2003:

'... Len quietly goes about his job. Taking pictures and talking to people. Given that this is the scope of what he does, it may seem hard to describe him as unique. He is. Len Grant is the only photographer in Manchester who, day-to-day, has made the rebuilding and regeneration of Manchester his subject... he gets amongst the people, from chief executives and cabinet ministers to site workers and soon-to-be-rehoused. He has an exhaustive and precious archive of Manchester in turnaround and the city is lucky to have him.'

Making Manchester 1990-2003

Exhibited at Cube Gallery, May-August 2003

30th June 2003: '... Feeling of euphoria beginning to wear off but I have a new lease of life with the Maine Road project and with New Islington and Ancoats back in the swing. Absolutely plenty to do. Money is still a worry. Thinking of going digital but all sorts of issues to consider: quality, security, pricing... still on antidepressants.'

After years of neglect, rumour and empty promises, the Cardroom estate in Ancoats was about to start its transformation into New Islington, English Partnerships' third project in its Millennium Community Programme.

The idea was to create more sustainable communities by bringing together new methods in planning, design and construction.

The Cardroom's housing design and urban layout were distinctive: short cul-de-sacs; houses only accessible by foot; bedrooms built over walkways.

The new residents arrived in the early 1980s, to their new houses next to the historic mills of Ancoats. They told of beautiful houses, landscaped pathways, benches on which to sit and watch the world go by. It was neighbourly too. Everyone knew each other; mothers lived near daughters, grandmothers near granddaughters.

Street names evoked the cotton industry in which many had worked: Spinning Jenny Walk, Weft Walk, Warp Walk, Finishing Walk. The estate got its name from the room in the mill where raw cotton was 'carded' or cleaned by large machines before spinning could begin.

By the time I was commissioned as 'documenter of change' in 2001, the Cardroom had been dubbed 'one of the worst estates in Manchester.'

COMMISSION:

New Islington 2001-10

Commissioned by The New Islington Client Group, with Urban Splash as lead developer

Published as Cardroom Voices, 2004 and From the Ground Up, 2007, by Len Grant Photography

It was about this time that I felt confident enough to describe myself as a 'photographer *and* writer'. In 1999 I had attended a journalism evening class at Manchester University taught by a diligent ex-hack. Write with passion, he encouraged. I practised my fledgling skills writing reviews of photographic exhibitions for *The Big Issue in the North*, often interviewing the artists. From then, I wrote more extensively for my own commissions, including New Islington. For a time, when I was documenting vulnerable lives for books or blogs (see p.138), I was considered more as a writer who took photographs rather than the other way round.

Cardroom estate, September 2001: 'As soon as I turned off the main road there was immediately a different feel about the place, something quite depressing. I pressed the button to lock all the car doors and immediately felt guilty. After working for many years in Hulme and Moss Side I knew that not everyone here was as threatening as that group of lads I'd just passed on the corner.

'I knew there were people here who couldn't move away, who were dependent on the council for their next relocation. I knew also that most didn't want to move; they had lived here all their lives and had good friends and family on their doorsteps. The houses and the environment might not be in great shape but there would be a community spirit – and a strong one at that – because they were all in it together.'

For Cardroom Voices, my first book about the creation of New Islington, I visited residents and listened to their experiences of living in the soon-to-be-demolished estate.

My subjects included Joan, right, and 10-year-old Raph who I photographed with his mates on the only green space available on which to play football.

I also gave Raph a disposable camera. His views of his neighbourhood, below, were insightful.

The 'football pitch' was subsequently earmarked for Islington Square (p.106) and, five years later, Raph, his mum and his sister moved into one of its new properties.

"I was born and bred in Ancoats. We lived at Garrick Street until I was 13 then we moved up to Newton Heath.

"Back then it was all two up, two downs. You'd walk into the lobby, then there was a parlour, then a living room and a kitchen. Upstairs were two bedrooms and outside there was toilet and a back yard.

"We were a big family. I was the fifth of eleven. Eight girls and three boys. My mam and dad used to sleep in the parlour and us eight girls would sleep in two beds in one bedroom and the boys in the other. There was no bedding, we'd just sleep under army coats. We didn't know what bedding was.

"There were no three-piece suites or anything then. We had a big wooden table. The kids would come in from school first and then we'd have our tea, then the big 'uns would have their tea. The same on Sunday.

"My dad used to work at Watmoughs making eyelets for shoes, and laces. It was only down the way, further down from Ancoats Hospital. Mam was a cleaner, she worked all over.

"I used to do barmaiding. It was at The Wrexham pub where they taught me barmaiding. Then when I came back here I did it at The Magpie, The Bank of England, The Crown and the Cob O'Coal."

Joan

Over several months the initially sceptical residents of the Cardroom met with the regeneration professionals in the empty Cob o'Coal pub. Sketches gave way to colourful plans and plans became 3D models.

"I think people need some loose ideas rather than starting completely from scratch. Because you're talking to a community that's never really had that level of consultation before and find it difficult to articulate what they want. But they find it easy to say, "Can you put that in, can you turn that around?" So they're able to respond to something put in front of them rather than sit down and say, "Where do we go from here?""

Emma Sneyd, community engagement officer for the New Islington consultation

"It's surprising what people leave behind. We find old clothing, things people have stored in their attics, birthday cards, old teddy bears, anything really. You find the odd coin but mainly it's rubbish.

"You often get photographs... and they're memories for people, aren't they? ... why do they leave them behind?"

"Yeah, it's my mam! And that's Karen and that's our Dee. That's not Drill Walk, it's Yarn Walk. 10 Yarn Walk. Ah, thanks, Len. When you're moving you don't realise how much you leave behind. It's really, really stressful. I left loads in that house, because this one is a lot smaller.

"Dee'd be about one and a half and Karen'd be five or six. I remember that photograph dead clear. That garden was massive. She was messing about with the kids, having a laugh and joke with them. You know, it's one of those days that sticks in your head.

"You were honoured when you got a visit from my mam. She'd only stay a few days because she's got a big family. There are eight of us. She'd stay with me, then she'd go to my sister's, then she'd go to my other sister's, then she'd go to my brother's and then go to London."

To serve the ever-growing city centre population at the beginning of the nineteenth century, the Ardwick and Ancoats Dispensary opened on Great Ancoats Street in 1828. By 1873 the Ancoats Hospital had opened and the two institutions amalgamated on Old Mill Street.

For the next 130 years the hospital served the community and all the local residents had stories of frantic dashes to casualty with injured children or siblings.

Sisters Joyce Cunliffe and Patty Hamilton live three doors away from each other on Weybridge Road, just yards from Ancoats Hospital.

Joyce: I was a cleaner in the kitchen. You know, stoves and chippers and that. She was on the pot machine.

Patty: It was lovely, a spotless hospital. Nobody could call that. I was there about 16 years.

Joyce: You were longer than me, weren't you? I was there about 12 years, I think.

Patty: I started on the cleaning first before I worked in the kitchen. And what a clean hospital that was. Every night you'd have to scrub the chairs the patients had sat on. You know, in casualty and outpatients. Spotless it was.

Joyce: Have you seen the state of the mop heads that they bring out in hospitals now?

Patty: It's a disgrace.

Joyce: We nearly pass out, don't we? Compared to what we've been used to. They've no idea of cleaning now, those cleaners.

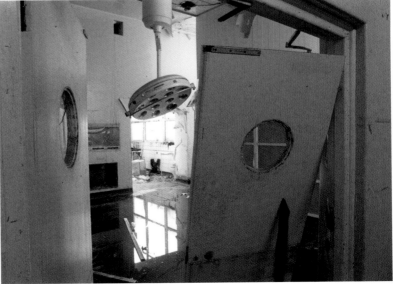

For this October 2003 view of the Cardroom estate, I was on the roof of the derelict nurses' accommodation at Ancoats Hospital before its demolition. Old Mill Street is in the foreground, the Ancoats mills beyond.

Taken from Murrays' Mills – looking in the opposite direction to the shot above – this June 2004 image shows the beginnings of the new canal arm that would ostensibly link the Rochdale and Ashton Canals.

The white-painted Cob o' Coal pub, venue for the community consultations, is on the far left and, in the background, Ancoats Hospital.

In the foreground the contractors have created a 'biopile' to remediate contaminated earth.

The plan had always been that New Islington would be a mixture of tenures: homes for sale alongside social housing.

The first phase of social housing – 23 new homes offered to those who'd had their homes demolished – was designed by FAT (Fashion, Architecture, Taste), a London practice renowned for their anti-modernist approach. Architect Charles Holland (left), told me: "The first consultation was quite chaotic, quite hair-raising as I recall. Fifteen people all talking at once, it was like walking into a wind tunnel! Although we'd done consultations before, this was more volatile because people were passionate about what was going on.

"That's when we decided to visit everyone in their own homes as if they were the client. Those visits were the best bit really. It allowed us to talk one-on-one and people were much more open. In those big meetings you get the same people saying things, which is great for them, but there's a lot of people who either don't come or just keep quiet."

Architect, Charles Holland at an early consultation, December 2004.

Islington Square during construction, May 2005 and, opposite, completed.

"It's an experience I've never had before. We were consulted at all levels: the interior design, the style of your cupboards, even down to the chrome handles, so that was a revelation in itself. I've moved house a few times and with a council property it's normally a case of, 'Here are the keys, take it or leave it.' Whereas Urban Splash have been great, I can't fault them.

"It will be better when the others have moved in round the back. There are people who I know. So it'll be a little community of 23 houses, all looking out for each other. No, I like it. There are one or two that are a bit sceptical yet, those that haven't moved in, but I think they'll change their minds once they're in."

Terry Sheldon, May 2006

In 2006 I was invited by The Lowry in Salford to stage an exhibition about my regeneration work in New Islington. I thought it might be interesting to extend the remit and see how other photographers were tackling the same subject.

So I, in turn, invited photographers Shaw + Shaw, who were working in Salford, and Liz Lock and Mishka Henner, who were documenting Hattersley in Tameside. 15-year-old Charlie Burns, a Hattersley resident and accomplished photographer who Liz and Mishka were mentoring, was also featured.

The exhibition introduction ran: 'It used to be called slum clearance, now it's called regeneration. Tens of thousands of families across Britain are experiencing the largest re-housing programme since the 1960s. So what's it like to be part of this brave new world?'

EXHIBITION:

**Our House
2006**

The Lowry, Salford Quays,
September-November 2006

With accompanying book
published by Len Grant
Photography

Photographer Len Grant from Withington has unveiled his latest exhibition at The Lowry. The exhibit, called Our House, is made from more than 2,000 prints of terraced houses across Manchester and Salford, presented on a nine meter-stretch of gallery wall. The exhibition is on now and will run until Sunday, November 19. For more information visit www.thelowry.com.

For Our House I made new portraits of the residents I had photographed four years earlier for the Cardroom Voices book. Some were now in their new homes, others had moved away, and some were still waiting to be re-housed.

I also shot a short film, In the Middle of our Street, where I recorded people's views of the terraced house. One wall of the exhibition was covered floor to ceiling with 2,300 6x4 inch prints of terraced houses around Manchester. It was my homage to the quintessential northern house type that was increasingly under threat from the controversial Housing Market Renewal programme.

Agnes Lewis was born at 24 Pollard Street East in Ancoats.

"I always remember the wallpaper, deep blue with great big red roses. I loved it.

"Opposite was Bazley's Mill, a great big mill. Every morning I woke up to the sound of the machine starting off and all the clogs coming up the street. It was marvellous."

She was born with polio and a deformed leg. Despite operations to straighten it, she had worn a calliper since she was a teenager.

"When I was 15 I started a sewing job at Lawrence's on Pollard Street. I've always tried to hide the fact I was lame, so I took the calliper off when I started there. To keep my secret this leg never touched the treadmill, I only used one leg. But there's been a lot of wear and tear over the years and that's what's caused the arthritis.

"I was always frightened of leaving Lawrence's in case somewhere else would realise I could only use one leg and wouldn't give me a job so I stayed there for 47 years."

I first photographed Agnes outside her back door in July 2002. She and her older sister Liz had moved to the house when it was new, after their parents had died. Neither had married. Later,

Agnes nursed Liz through Alzheimer's before she died in 1993.

The Cardroom was being demolished around her, and other residents were moving into temporary accommodation. She, however, decided she'd wait until Guest Street – the second phase of the social housing – was complete, so she'd only have to move once.

I'd pop in to see Agnes often as I walked around the estate, capturing the stages of demolition. She was practically housebound and was happy to make a brew and have some company. Agnes loved her cats and had acquired a number over the years. Mostly they were strays that stuck around, enjoying her hospitality.

By March 2007 her bungalow was ready and, on the day of the move, I arrived early to document the occasion. One neighbour was pulling up flowers in her garden to transplant across the way. Most of her furniture had already gone and she sat in an empty living room surrounded by cat baskets.

"I had three cats. Two of them were safely packed away but I didn't know where the little 'un had gone, upstairs somewhere. When the men came to get my suite, the door was left open and poor little Bobby flew out and I never saw him again.

"Then I came over to Guest Street... oh.... it was all laid out lovely: the curtains and carpets I'd picked; all my old furniture was there, it was just like what I'd left in Spinning Jenny Walk. But I was tired, really tired. I thought, this was it, I'm finished... if I last another week it'll be a miracle. I felt desperate. It must have been six or eight weeks when I really felt down."

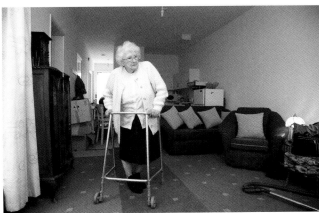

Even after my New Islington commission came to an end, I'd still pop in on Agnes if I was nearby. I'd change a light bulb or run an errand. When she complained of not being able to do her regular crossword, I organised a trip to the in-store optician at Asda at Eastlands where she enjoyed her first ever trip around the aisles in a mobility scooter.

In 2011, Agnes was diagnosed with cancer. After a spell in hospital, she was cared for at home by agency nurses, friends and neighbours before she died on July 12th. She was 87. I was invited to deliver a eulogy at her funeral:

'Despite not having family of her own, Agnes has enjoyed the friendship that you lot, her Ancoats neighbours, give automatically without thinking. For Agnes, it's been more than keeping an eye out for her: *you* have been her family, and there aren't many places left where that would happen. On behalf of Agnes, let me pay tribute and say thank you to you all.

'So Agnes, you were a lovely lady and I will miss you. Your good friends and neighbours will miss you and Ancoats will miss you too.'

By October 2007, steady progress had been made at New Islington.
Cotton Field, the new water park, was complete, although not yet
connected to the Rochdale Canal in front of the Ancoats Mills.
Residents had spent their first twelve months in their new homes
at the playfully-designed Islington Square (centre, background).
Although not universally admired, the bold social housing put a
marker down for what might follow.

In the centre, the Ancoats Primary Care Centre was complete and
Old Mill Street, with its distinctive angled lamposts, was very nearly
open again for traffic.

Chips, Will Alsop's first residential building in the UK, was under
construction next to the Ashton Canal, far right. Unseen, behind
the jagged roof of Stubbs Mill, Agnes had settled into her new
bungalow on Guest Street.

New Islington

Towards the end of its 80-year tenure, Maine Road football ground, squeezed between the terraced streets of Moss Side, had grown to resemble an over-sized cuckoo chick squatting in the wrong nest.

Although precious to generations of sky blue fans, the crumbling ground could no longer accommodate a top flight club and a deal was struck to relocate to the City of Manchester Stadium across town.

Such was the fans' devotion to Maine Road that an auction of fixtures and fittings attracted hundreds back to the ground one Sunday morning, all keen to claim at least one piece of Manchester City history. In the early part of the commission I followed up those purchases, photographing fans across the city with their memorabilia.

I've always enjoyed photographing demolition – the machines, the mess, the workers – but at Maine Road the story was always going to be about the social and economic impact its demise would have on the local community. The chippies and local shops would suffer but, I wondered before I began, would nearby residents be happy to see the stadium go?

Maine Road football ground 2003-04

Commissioned by Manchester City Council

Published as Full Time at Maine Road, by Len Grant Photography, 2004

My first rolls of film were of Manchester City's last game at Maine Road. They lost 1-2 to Southampton.

"People are so emotionally connected to this place. I recognise the same faces week after week. They've been coming to Maine Road for years. It's part of their lives and it's hard to break with tradition."

Maine Road football ground

Lot 70: Final bid £40
Chris O'Connor, engineer, Wythenshawe

Lot 54: Final bid £50
Nick Heaton with Jacob, company director, Cheadle Hulme

Lots 398-432: Final bid £25
Wesley Reeves with Maya, Sale

Lot 65: Final bid £75
Andrew Dowdall, plumber, Wythenshawe

"I can go right back. I was born in Wansford Street.
My grandparents lived at No.3 and we lived at No.11.
My grandad and my mum used to take in bikes.
We were a big family and my dad wasn't in good
health so it was extra for my mum and pocket money
for my grandad.

"We only charged 3d a bike and we'd pack them into
our back yard and a couple of our neighbours' back
yards as well. Then we had to mind them all through
the match. If there were any tandems we'd have a go
on them up and down the back entry."

Dorothy Jones

Maine Road football ground

'We'd look forward to a Saturday. There was always a lot of excitement with all the police, the cars, the horses, the customers. The whole area was alive. Everyone was excited.

'We had some wonderful customers, this was their regular. Some said that even their great-grandfathers used to come here. We had a group from Norway who'd fly over for every game and come and eat here first.

'But now the buzz has gone. We've lost a lot of business. One match was equivalent to a week's takings. So imagine 20 home matches a year, we've lost 20 extra weeks in takings. The shop was struggling during the week but the matches saved us.'

Sue and Essey Saeli

rwsdesk: 834 9677. Deliveries: 246 1273. Leaflet Services: 475 4808   Manchester Metro News Friday, November 26, 200

Len captures final throes of a legend

by Simon Donohue

THE dramatic end of an era at Manchester City's Maine Road ground has been captured for the history books by celebrated documentary photographer Len Grant.

Images and interviews taken during the 16-month demolition process are included in a new book, entitled Full Time at Maine Road, which was launched on Tuesday night.

The book, commissioned by Manchester Council, begins with the final Manchester City home games at Maine Road and ends with the striking image of a pile of rubble standing on the site where countless of the Blues' famous clashes took place over the years.

Although not a football fan himself, 44-year-old Len said working on the book gave him a unique insight to the passion and emotions of the game.

He added: "One mother and daughter from Rochdale came to visit twice a week during the demolition process.

"They would walk all the way around the ground.

"For them it was clearly part of the process of letting go, part of the grieving process."

The book marks yet another amazing achievement for Len who did not turn his hand to full-time professional photography until 1990 when the Withington father-of-three's first professional assignment was for a double glazing and conservatory company based on the Wirral.

Having taken documentary-type images as an amateur, Mr Grant's skills in the field were quickly recognised.

Other assignments include charting building work at the Manchester Evening News Arena and Bridgewater Hall sites.

Len said: "I do feel we are capturing part of history.

"I remember former council

LAST DAYS: Maine Road's main stand, one of the pictures in Len Grant's (right) book

leader and Blackley MP Graham Stringer saying there is only one picture of the town hall being built. Once the process of demolition or construction takes place, there's absolutely no going back."

'I have sat here for the last three days enthralled in your book. In parts I have cried because seeing Maine Road being pulled down brick by brick is hard to look at. But, then again, you have still captured the beauty of the place I will always love.

'I do hope that one day I can come to love Eastlands as much as I have loved Maine Road.'

Emma, December 2004

In July 2002 I photographed thousands of spectators walking up the Ashton New Road or along the adjacent canal path to watch the XVII Commonwealth Games play out on the reclaimed site of a old colliery in Beswick, east Manchester.

Few of those spectators would have been aware of the incredible turnaround they were a part of.

Up until the 1970s east Manchester was a manufacturing powerhouse: railway engines, chemicals, machinery, pumps, aircraft. Jobs were plentiful. The place teemed with people. Pubs were on every street corner.

The decline was slow and deep. By the time the Council had secured funds for the area's revival in 1999, its housing, health, employment, education and crime issues were entrenched. It would be an uphill struggle.

I arrived late to the story. In 2004 I put a proposal forward to the regeneration agencies – New Deal for Communities (NDC) and New East Manchester Ltd – to produce a series of large-format magazines that would follow the area's social as well as physical revival. The success of this regeneration project was underpinned by a genuine inclusion of local people in all aspects of decision making, and that engagement was reflected in my documentation.

We may look at areas like Ancoats or projects like The Bridgewater Hall as exemplars of Manchester's regeneration. But for me, the neighbourhood work in east Manchester is more significant. In a few short years residents who were once fearful of leaving their homes reclaimed their neighbourhoods. A desperate feeling of powerlessness was replaced by cooperation with those in charge. Initiatives piloted here were replicated throughout the city and beyond.

COMMISSION:

East Manchester
2004-10

Commissioned by
New Deal for Communities
and New East Manchester Ltd

Ten issues of East magazine,
a 45-post blog
(www.thisiseast.com), and
Reclaiming East Manchester:
Ten Years of Resident-led
Regeneration, published by
Len Grant Photography,
2010

"Before 1999 you could never get an answer from the Town Hall, on anything. NDC has empowered us to challenge the Council on the services they deliver, and that's worked."

Irene Baron, resident.

East Manchester

Inspired by *Reportage*, an international magazine of photojournalism, graphic designer Alan Ward and I, produced a dummy edition of East magazine to illustrate our ideas.

At 28 pages, and with a format larger than A4, it would give us the opportunity to showcase my photography and develop some extended picture stories.

My initial proposal had included upskilling local writers to become contributors but that didn't come off. Instead, as well as the articles I wrote myself, I commissioned pieces from freelance writers. Jonathan Schofield, Phil Griffin, Louise Tickle and Mark Hillsdon were amongst them.

Free to residents, the first edition of East came out in February 2005 and, until November 2009, Alan and I produced ten issues, with over 50 local articles. Issue One included the construction of the B of the Bang (see next page); the economic upturn for local pubs following Manchester City's return to east Manchester; and a profile of Ancoats' carnival costume-maker, Peddy Herbert.

For the final issue, I spent time with a youth cycle team at the Velodrome; spoke with teenagers combatting negative media portrayals and, with my camera and tape recorder, explored Holt Town, an area earmarked for new family housing.

East won a 'Best Use of Image' Award at the 2005 SUN [Shot Up North] Awards; the magazine category in the McNaughton Design and Print Awards, 2008; and was shortlisted twice in the media category of the NW Business Environment Awards.

The print edition was followed by a blog in 2008 and for the next two years I produced dozens more articles about east Manchester's continuing success.

THE ADVERTISER   ☎ 0161 223 9199   www.nemadvertiser.co.uk

Regeneration story told in pictures

EAST Manchester has its own pictorial record of the area's regeneration, with the launch of East magazine.

The thrice-yearly magazine aims to tell the ongoing stories behind Britain's biggest regeneration programme, and is illustrated by the stunning pictures of Len Grant.

Len spent the majority of 2004 capturing images including the demolition of Manchester City's former Maine Road home. The magazine covers Ancoats, Miles Platting, Newton Heath, Beswick, Bradford, Clayton, Openshaw and Gorton.

The first issue has an insight into the B of the Bang sculpture, and landlords explain the impact of City's home matches on local watering holes. There is a walk down Memory Lane with Clayton's 103-year-old resident Elizabeth Wells, and Paddy Herbert's work making costumes for the East Feast parade features.

The launch issue has been published by Len Grant Photography and sponsored by English Partnerships, whose regional director, Paul Spooner, said: "English Partnerships is proud to support East. There's a host of regeneration activity taking place in East Manchester and this publication will help tell that story, by celebrating the people and places at the very heart of it."

Tom Russell, New East Manchester Chief Executive, said: "East is a visually stunning publication which is a must for everyone interested in East Manchester."

Available in selected shops, it costs £3.

LEN Grant and Tom Russell take a look at the East magazine.
MI082305

east

Still Making It
East Expo
The Hidden Gem
Pace Setters

the magazine about regeneration in east manchester   three pounds

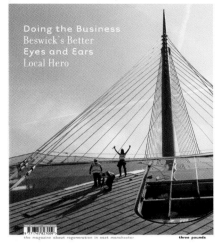

east

Doing the Business
Beswick's Better
Eyes and Ears
Local Hero

the magazine about regeneration in east manchester   three pounds

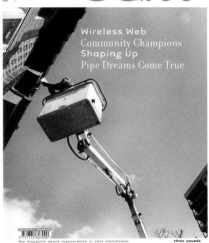

east

Wireless Web
Community Champions
Shaping Up
Pipe Dreams Come True

the magazine about regeneration in east manchester   three pounds

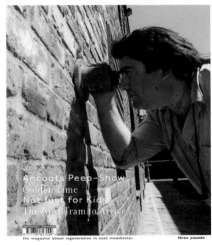

east

Ancoats Peep-Show
Golden Time
Not Just for Kids
The Next Tram to Arrive...

the magazine about regeneration in east manchester   three pounds

east

Dying Days
Powerhouse to Penthouse
Newcomers
Get on That Bus!

the magazine about regeneration in east manchester   three pounds

east

Comedy Divas
Gothic Revival
Bang On!
Listen Up
It's Good To Talk

the magazine about regeneration in east manchester

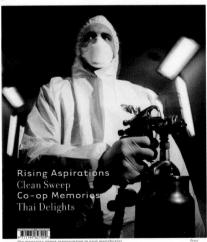

east

Rising Aspirations
Clean Sweep
Co-op Memories
Thai Delights

the magazine about regeneration in east manchester   free

east

Wish You Were Here?
Miles Better for Jobs
Pieces of the Past

the magazine about regeneration in east manchester   free

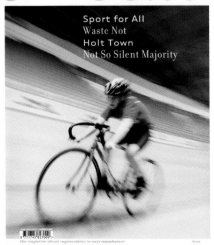

east

Sport for All
Waste Not
Holt Town
Not So Silent Majority

the magazine about regeneration in east manchester   free

I got to know the B of the Bang well. I photographed its core being fabricated in a Sheffield foundry and, early one Sunday morning, captured its arrival through the streets of east Manchester on a lowloader. For six months I trained my lens skywards as its 180 hollow steel spikes were welded into place. At 56 metres, it became the UK's largest sculpture and a symbol for the area's revival.

The artwork was inspired by sprinter Linford Christie, who started, not on the bang of the starting pistol, but on the b of the bang. On 12th January 2005, Christie joined creator, Thomas Heatherwick and east Manchester schoolkids to celebrate its completion. Four months later a spike, hanging loose, had to be cut off by firefighters.

After much finger-pointing, 'de-construction' began in April 2009. It was the only structure I'd photographed going up and coming down.

They were in the long queue at the Crusty Cob, the legendary pie shop on Beswick Street.

Minimum 22% meat.

She was ahead of the other two in a small pink skirt and an even smaller top that covered only half of a pregnant belly.

Beware very hot surface.

It was hot outside and in. She must have been incredibly uncomfortable. The two lads, a few behind her in the line, were giving her some friendly banter, trying to embarrass her.

Once served, they stepped out onto the pavement and opened their paper bags. She would be amazing to photograph. I could never pluck up the courage to ask. What would I say? How would they react?

They strolled around the corner into Pollard Street and I ate my pie watching them disappear into the estate.

My lunch finished, I got into my car and followed them. They could only say no. Maybe not very graciously, but they could only turn me down. I reached the junction with Bradford Road but they'd disappeared between some houses. I took a left and then a right, and there they were.

I can't remember exactly what I said. Something about thinking her stomach was very photogenic. Which one of you is the dad? When is it due? Must be soon. I do a lot of regeneration work around here and could I take your picture?

Yeah, okay.

The soon-to-be father lived on the next street. They walked round and I parked up outside. He quite rightly quizzed me about my photography. Why do you want to take this picture? What's it for? I showed them my Cardroom Voices book. Luckily he knew Raph. That was enough recommendation.

June 2005

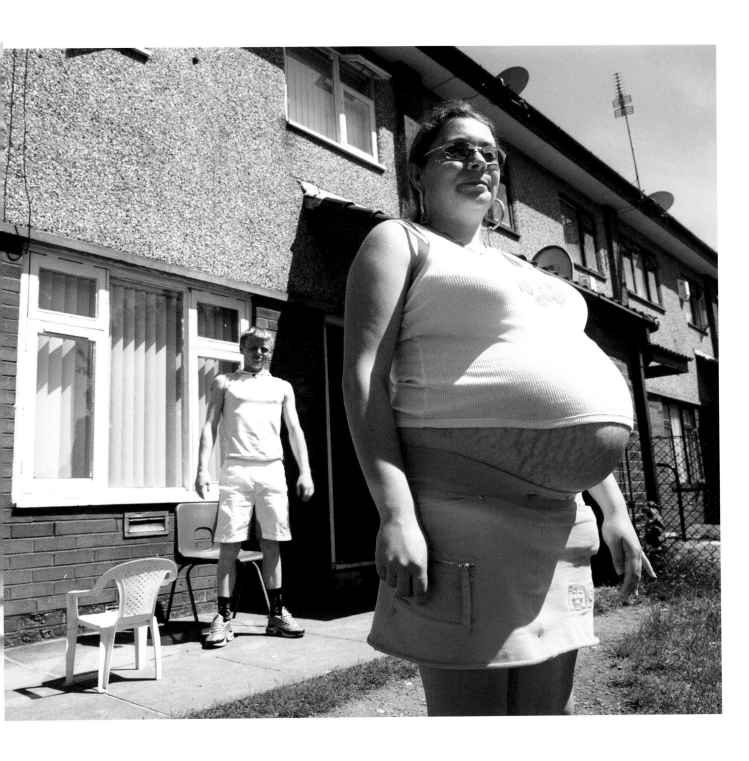

East Manchester

I enjoyed a fair amount of creative freedom with East magazine. I suggested most of the story ideas, choosing subjects I knew would look good in the large format. But there was a desire to do something more. Here was a huge swathe of the city in transition and I was keen to record it in a way that was more personal than the commissioned work. A new project was emerging.

Around this time I'd begun using a digital camera and, although I appreciated the advantages, I was keen to return to film to employ a slower approach. If shooting digitally was like firing a shotgun, then I wanted to get back to being a sniper.

I decided I'd take all the images for this new project on my Mamiya twin lens camera, the sort you hold at waist level and look down into. The camera gives a large, square negative and so it became, to me at least, the 'Square Project'.

As so often, I struggled with an approach. I'd decided on a methodology before formulating a clear strategy and then searched everywhere for inspiration. In May 2005, I watch a TV programme about American photographer Stephen Shore's 1970s road trip with a large format camera. 'That's it,' I wrote that night in my notebook, 'a road trip across east Manchester.' Later that month, a book by Magda Segal caught my attention. 'Perhaps I'm trying to be too clever, too ambitious. Maybe it should be an East Manchester at Home project like London at Home: people in their living rooms and kitchens. Not much text, just them.'

I took seven rolls of film between August and November 2005. Photographs of boarded up terraces and kids knocking a ball against the gable end contrasted with new flats, new roads, a new fast food restaurant.

It would be another three years before I returned to the Square Project. The Our House exhibition at The Lowry, and another New Islington book, were just some of the distractions. I took some portraits, keen to meet people in the street, and strike up conversations. Below is Angela, her niece Jodie and 10-month-old Cole at Grey Mare Lane Market. "I've been 30 years coming to this market," she told me.

Despite writing about it enthusiastically in May 2010 – 'there will only be a few years it will be like this' – the Square Project is incomplete after a total of 18 rolls of film over five years. It never had a clear objective, other than documenting change, and none of these images have ever been published, or even discussed with friends. The experience, however, is not totally wasted. In a page of my notebook I considered a new idea: 'the anatomy of a failed photography project'.

'The first two cities on earth to be connected by passenger railway service were Manchester and Liverpool. A thankless act,' wrote Phil Griffin for our collaboration to mark Architecture Week, 2005.

'However it has been spun out and replicated across the world, the viaduct that springs from London Road towards Edge Hill and Lime Street is of the first order. The enormous brick arches that stomped on Little Ireland and marched through Knott Mill and Cornbrook to Pomona signal modern globalisation.

'This City Wall attempts to rout out a familiar structure that the city may just have grown to hold in contempt. We do not argue its grace or beauty, but we loudly celebrate its place.'

This City Wall 2005

with Phil Griffin

Displayed at Manchester Piccadilly Railway Station

Encouraged by Phil, I photographed 176 railway arches, running from Piccadilly to Pomona, which made up the inner city viaduct that he compared to the Roman walls of York and Chester. The images were displayed as a 44-metre exhibition running the length of Platform 12 at Manchester Piccadilly. It was only supposed to be up for six weeks, it stayed for over a year.

"The first arches would have been built in the 1840s," I said to the *Manchester Evening News* journalist, "at a time when the Town Hall had not even been built.

"They would have been some of the tallest structures in Manchester and people would've come from all over to see them. There were no planning regulations in those days and the arches would have been built right through residential terraced areas."

EXHIBITION WITH A DIFFERENCE FROM AN ARCH-ENTHUSIAST

M.E.N. Friday, July 1, 2005

DISPLAY . . . Len Grant with some of the images of arches on show

Picture: DAVE THOMPSON

In 2006 designer Alan Ward and I collaborated with engineer Martin Stockley on an unorthodox monograph following his considerable but unseen contribution to the city's regeneration (p.170).

When The Reluctant Engineer was published, Martin's client, Town Centre Securities, decided they wanted a book too – one that would follow the renovation of the oldest surviving warehouse in Manchester.

Dale Street Warehouse, as it was then known, sat on the edge of Piccadilly Basin and was home to a bathroom and tile emporium. On each floor, baths, basins, shower trays and vanity units snuggled up incongruously against 200-year-old cast-iron columns.

Unlike previous construction commissions there were no huge vistas of the site, no towering cranes, no matrix of steel beams. This would be a chronicle of the craft of stone masons, timber specialists, roofers, joiners and glazers.

Martin Stockley Associates managed the renovation project and subsequently leased the upper two floors, while encouraging inward investment agency Marketing Manchester to occupy the basement and ground.

COMMISSION:

Carver's Warehouse 2006-08

Commissioned by
Town Centre Securities

Privately published in 2008
as Carver's Warehouse

Here was a building made in 1806 during the reign of George III; at a time when work had just begun on the Arc de Triomphe in Paris and Beethoven was composing his Violin Concerto in D. Most significantly perhaps, it was the year in which Isambard Kingdom Brunel was born, one of the men who was to have an extraordinary impact on the nineteenth century and all that followed.

From Martin Stockley's afterword to the Carver's Warehouse book

Perhaps my greatest pleasure has been for my practice to have managed the construction works. To have our hands on the transformation of this dormant giant of a building was a privilege. We have purposely taken a very gentle approach to the historic fabric, not over-cleaning, leaving the signs of past activity where it does not prevent the new...

... It has been a head gardener role for me, with my team there every day, leading and guiding the process and able to see and affect the minute daily changes as the potential of the building blossoms before our eyes.

Martin Stockley

Looking back through my notebooks, there was one project idea that rumbled on for many years, each entry assessing the pros and cons of taking it forward.

7th May 2000: 'I like the idea of doing something in contrast to the PR side of Manchester that I'm mostly portraying. A project about the deprivation in the city. The City of Manchester is up there amongst the highest in child poverty etc. There is something there to do. What and how, I haven't quite resolved.'

10th November 2001: 'What do I want to say? I want to counter all the positive stories/pictures I've been making in the city centre. See the other side of the coin to the new loft apartments, trendy bars and restaurants. There are parts of our city that are so close geographically to the centre and yet miles away in terms of prosperity. What about the conflict of the middle-class, middle-aged man documenting working-class neighbourhoods? This is just an excuse for NOT doing it.'

Three years on, it was still a thought in my notebooks, but I was continually looking for inspiration, a way in. At a Robert Frank retrospective at Tate Modern I came away with more questions than answers.

29th December 2004: 'Frank talks about 'finding the story'. It comes from the picture story ethos of the magazines where they have a distinct beginning, middle and end. Would that work? This year at Manchester Art Gallery, Mary Ellen Mark talked about repeatedly photographing the same people over a period of time. That sounds a good approach.'

At the beginning of the following year, I thought I'd come up with a solution.

15th January 2005: 'It came to me today as I was driving to the IWMN [Imperial War Museum North] to see Paula Keenan's show. Rather than trying to do it all myself... get into collaboration with someone locally, a young person, mentor someone, train them into how to take photographs so they could be documenting at a time I couldn't. I'm thinking about Toxteth Street in Openshaw. But how would I find such a person?'

13th February 2005: 'The aim is to give people a voice, to act as a conduit between people who are not normally heard and the people who don't normally hear them. It's not a judgement on them, or on better off people, it's simply a line of communication from one part of the community to another.'

It was another two years before there's something of a breakthrough.

19th April 2007: 'The project is back in my sights. It's the one about poverty/social exclusion. In January, Mishka and Liz, Jo and Christoph and I met up for a debrief on the Our House project and I kind of came out about wanting to do this project. That was it. I'd let it be vocalised so I then had to do something. So I contacted Libby Graham at New Deal and she was absolutely all for it, whatever 'it' is, and said she'd help me make contacts.

'But there are lots of accounts of lives on the edge (I'm reading Bernard Hare, Fergal Keane). What's going to be so special about mine? I like the idea of following a young person, a child, over a period of years to see where they are at. Labour have pledged to eradicate child poverty by 2020 but no one believes they will, and they're not on target. So, how do I do it? How do I approach a disadvantaged family and say, 'I'd like to photograph you because you are poor?''

The following month I was introduced to the director of a local charity that supports 'chaotic families' and subsequently spent a morning photographing one family in Beswick (below) but the mother stopped answering my texts. My potential subjects had challenging lives and the demands of a photographer were not a priority.

I become despondent again but then, in the autumn of 2007, I read Magnum photographer David Hurn, *On Being a Photographer*, writing about false starts. I decided I needed a new strategy and wrote a list of all the people I knew who might offer me an 'in' – act as a bridge between me and my potential subjects. There were seven contacts, I know now that one was productive.

Six months on, in March 2008, I was sitting in a drug user's flat in Ashton. "Would you like a cup of tea?" asked Billy, minutes after injecting himself.

Billy is now in his 30s and has been a heroin addict all his adult life. But he's had enough. Taking my interest in him as an incentive to come through a tough detox and rehabilitation programme, he allows me into his life before and after drugs. Success rates are depressingly low and Billy has tried before to get clean.

Billy is one of three people I 'follow' for over twelve months, documenting the twists and turns as they try to get themselves sorted.

As I note at the time, I find it impossible to remain an objective observer. My intervention ultimately impacts on their lives, as they do on mine.

PROJECT:

**Billy and Rolonde
2008-09**

Published in 2010 by
Len Grant Photography

I'm early and it takes a while for the door to be opened. Maybe Billy is checking me out on the security camera he's set up in his bathroom window. When the door opens he is apologetic; he's overslept. His flatmate stays under the covers in the bedroom they share as Billy pulls on his trainers and find his jacket. It's payday and some of the pay is going on a fix.

Heading towards the main road Billy is in talkative mood, happy to answer my questions about his addiction. 'I spend between £20 and £40 a week on heroin – two or three hits – out of about £60 or £70 a week I get from the dole. I'm probably what they call a Gyro-junkie because I don't thieve to feed my addiction any more,' he says as we walk to the post office on the other side of the small estate.

There's a queue of six or seven waiting outside the post office. Billy acknowledges the two men and one woman in front of us: fellow users eager to draw their weekly benefit.

Barbara, a 70-year-old Zimbabwean asylum seeker becomes increasingly depressed as she's moved from one shared house to another, trying to stay afloat on the £35 a week in vouchers given to 'failed' asylum seekers.

Barbara is led inside and I follow. What should have been a reasonably-sized front room has been partitioned into a smaller room and a corridor. A woman carrying a vacuum cleaner squeezes past us as we step inside. In the room there is a single bed, a narrow wardrobe, a small chest of four drawers, two with broken handles, a black plastic chair, a mirror, and a row of five hooks. It is small and bleak, but it is on the ground floor and close to the area Barbara is familiar with.

'Is this OK for you?' asks the man from the accommodation provider.

'Yes,' says Barbara.

Middle-aged Allan is about the same age as me but our lives could not be more different. Some weeks drunk, some weeks sober, only the support of a voluntary group keeps Allan from going under altogether. "I'm still drinking and I don't care," he confides. "I'm going to die and I don't care."

Allan's enjoying being the tour guide. 'What do you think of today? Has it been all right for you?' he asks as we visit more bushes, more brambles. Is he worried that I'm shocked at what he's showing me, or concerned that the tour isn't coming up to my expectations?

Before we go into a café, there's a short diversion as Allan shows me where he's slept most recently. There's bedding and a broken umbrella amongst the litter. 'If it's dry, I'll sleep with the duvet over me. If it's wet, I'm on the duvet with the plastic sheet on top. The umbrella's for when it gets really bad.'

There were ten years between that initial notebook
scribble back in May 2000 and the launch of
Billy and Rolonde. Once it was published the
book proved to be a turning point. Through the
first person commentary and the long-term
collaboration, I'd introduced a storytelling style
that I developed in a subsequent book commission
(The Reclaim Book, p 172) and a series of blogs.
There were, of course, doubts.

6th April 2010: 'What next after Billy and Rolonde?

I'd like to get commissioned to do work around
social exclusion by charities etc in the same way I
get commissioned now to do regeneration work.

'Doesn't that immediately make it non-personal,
and therefore against everything I need to do with
this sort of thing?'

Allan signing books at the launch of Billy and Rolonde, April 2010

Billy & Rolonde

In 2009 I got into blogging. It was an ideal medium: a way of telling stories direct to the viewer or reader with little cost and no editor or curator in the middle.

My first was about east Manchester, a sequel to the successful – but expensive – East magazine series. A personal project about a teenage mum from Moss Side followed. Her First Year documented 17-year-old Frances who, on the arrival of her daughter Mia, had to leave her alcoholic mother's house – her childhood home – to live in supported accommodation in another part of the city.

Frances' own upbringing had been challenging. Her home life was chaotic, she was well known to Social Services and didn't get to school that often. We'd got to know each other through the inspirational Reclaim project (p.172) that supported disadvantaged young people.

PROJECT:

**Her First Year
2011-12**

Published as a 61-post blog:
www.herfirstyear.co.uk

The Her First Year blog, written by both Frances and me, tells the story of her first 12 months as a mum, determined to give her daughter a different childhood to her own.

It was a huge success. Frances got excited to learn that she had readers around the world – many of them single mothers – awaiting each new update. It won Best Personal Blog at the 2012 Blog North Awards and *The Guardian*'s *Weekend* magazine published a nine-page feature.

As we approached Mia's first birthday, Frances commented that she didn't want the blog to end. I felt the same.

29th February 2012: 'Daniel Meadows' talk at Redeye. He spoke of documenting someone else's life: 'Predator or Collaborator'. I'd been struggling with this for some time, and there it was on the screen.'

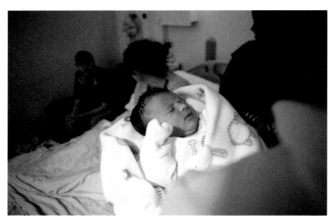

Inside, as Hassan puts Mia on Frances's knee, I tell
Frances what I have planned for a birthday present.
"I'm going to make a book of pictures from Her First
Year. But I want to include the birthday party. So you
won't get it until later. Is that okay?"

"Oh, wicked," she says and then, looking down to Mia,
"now don't try and climb off me.

"There are only about four maybe five pictures that
got taken of me when I was growing up," she says
abruptly. "I don't have any pictures of me as a baby.
There's a picture of me when I was about four, and
one of my brothers has got one of us all together.
And I've got one of me when I'm about seven, sat
with my brother."

"Why did you never have any photographs?
Was there never a camera?"

"No. Mum never even bought my school pictures.
I remember, when I got into year six I thought, enough
is enough. I'd always wanted one and, do you know
the ones they put in the classroom window so all the
parents can see, well I waited until after school and
I nicked them because I didn't have one single picture
of me in that school."

In 2012 Home Secretary Teresa May introduced the controversial 'hostile environment' policy towards migrants living in the UK without leave to remain. Ill-considered and inhumane, it caused suffering to many and did little to encouarge May's goal of voluntary repatriation.

As a result, a charitable foundation based in London – the Paul Hamlyn Foundation – launched a long-term project examining the lack of rights for undocumented migrant families. They were the unseen, the unprotected, the most vulnerable.

My year-long blog – Life Without Papers – told stories of three families in Manchester and Salford. I discovered parallel lives, people with nothing and no means of getting anything; an underworld where the struggle for the basics of food and shelter were constant.

I learnt a lot about inequality over those months and tried to convey that to the blog's readers. My interaction with my subjects was not dispassionate. How could it be? Even now my family and I remain friends with one mother and her daughter from that project.

In 2014 I wrote a screenplay of the blog after teaming up with theatre producer Alex Summers at The Royal Exchange Theatre. We workshopped the play in the theatre's studio and later adapted it as a one-person piece for the Re:Play Festival at The Lowry.

COMMISSION:

Life Without Papers 2012-13

Commissioned by Paul Hamlyn Foundation and Unbound Philanthropy

Published as a 43-post blog, currently with restricted access

Winner, Best Writing, Blog North Awards 2013.

Shortlisted in the digital innovation category of the Amnesty International Media Awards 2013.

Winner of a Speaking Together Media Award 2013.

31st August 2012: 'I have to admit to myself that I am feeling out of sorts.

It's about work, obviously. It's about the amount of work I have on, and the new projects I'm getting off the ground. It's about wanting to do a really good project on the undocumented for PHF and feeling nervous about that. And it's about being able to write again. I've had too long a break which has made me reverse in self confidence.

'Maybe I'm doing what I've always done: confusing stress with excitement. Maybe I'm excited about my new project but don't realise it.'

For twelve months I was 'embedded' at an advice centre on a low income Bolton housing estate. I researched and wrote stories from the sharp end of welfare reform and government austerity cuts, stories that every politician should hear. The blog highlighted the personal, compassionate support that three housing association staff – and their collaborators – continue to offer an ever-growing clientele.

COMMISSION:

As Rare As Rubies 2013-14

Commissioned by Bolton at Home

Published as a 42-post blog www.asrareasrubies.org

In this post from October 2013 I accompany trainee nurse Kellyann as she picks her son up from nursery. On the way she tells me she was suffering from postnatal depression when a friend dragged her along to a knitting group at the UCAN.

The school gate is opened and we walk round to the classroom entrance. "What would you have done, if the UCAN hadn't been here?"

"I'd be stuck. I'd have still been ill for a start. I know it was only knitting but it got me back out talking to people and it gave me something to look forward to. I started to go out – I'd had agoraphobia – and I started talking to the mums at the school gate. I came off my medication, finished my therapy, started and finished an access course with brilliant marks, then got one of 60 places at uni from over 1,800 applicants."

"Would you put starting your university degree down to walking into the UCAN?"

"Absolutely," she says as a nearby three-year-old is reunited with his mother and is immediately handed a chocolate egg. "UCAN fired the starting pistol for me."

Jackson is delighted to see his mum and unfazed by the stranger with her. "Can we go to the shop?" he asks, glancing at his classmate unwrapping the egg.

"Not today mate."

The centre – an Urban Care And Neighbourhood (UCAN) centre – is sandwiched between a chippy and a mini mart in Breightmet, Bolton.

Winner, Best City and Neighbourhood Blog, Blog North Awards 2014.

When I first read about the imminent construction of The Co-operative Group's new head office I thought it would make a great book. So, early in 2011 I dropped a boxful of my previous publications at their reception and waited.

18th March 2011: 'Have heard from the Co-op, they want a meeting...'

6th May 2011: 'Had been getting really quite down this week about lack of future work and so have been writing off to people. Then yesterday I heard that the Co-op head office project looks like it's a go-er, so well pleased about that.'

COMMISSION:

1 Angel Square, The Co-operative's new head office 2011-13

Commissioned by
The Co-operative Group

Published as 1 Angel Square
by Manchester University
Press, 2013

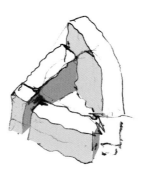

With flexibility a priority, architects 3DReid, at one stage, suggested three separate buildings joined at the corners. Rejected by the client, this morphed into one homogenous shape that eventually became 1 Angel Square.

Since the 2008 financial crisis my regeneration commissions had dried up and I was keen to get back on site.

As the latest building on the Co-op campus, and the first of the NOMA development, there was a fascinating story to tell. Not just about the historic site – Richard Arkwright built the world's first industrial-scale factory close by – and the Group's rationale for staying in the city; but also about the design evolution and the building's ground-breaking sustainability credentials. It would be powered by rapeseed oil grown on the Co-op's own farms.

I was commissioned to research and write the story as well as photograph the construction of a bold and beautiful building.

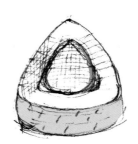

3rd July 2012: 'Big idea: a retrospective book.
Been reading through some of my own notebooks
and there are loads of bits of writing: thoughts,
ideas, worries, estimates, drafts of this and that
that would work really well together. They form
a kind of history of Manchester's redevelopment
over the last 25 years and give insight into a
creative thought process and the ups and downs of
being a freelancer.

They, I think, are an interesting read and would
make a great 25-year book. It should be called
'Unfinished Business' and sections would be bound
together but there'd be no cover, to suggest there is
more to come.

Really tight copy; in columns; small pictures.
A book to really delve into. My legacy book.'

The 1 Angel Square project was intense, but rewarding. As well as visiting the site every two weeks or so to photograph the construction, I also interviewed many of the professionals and heard the inside story of the building's development for the book text I was writing. This insight was different from other projects. I felt a deeper connection to 1 Angel Square and, like others, a peculiar sense of ownership as it took shape.

It seems everyone working on this project – the client, architects, engineers, construction professionals – all knew they were working on something unique. For many, it would be a career highlight.

My commission was to follow Trafford Council's transformation programme as it renovated its Grade II listed Town Hall, replaced its extension and leapt into the 21st century with a contemporary environment and a 'smarter way' of working.

An open brief from 5plus architects and 'access all areas' allowed me to follow the process as I wished. I set out, then, to record some of the more intriguing twists and turns of the construction and renovation process, the minutiae that might otherwise go unnoticed. On site I got up close to the skilled craftsmen refurbishing stone or replacing lead. Off site I documented time-served joiners constructing new oak benches for the council chamber and, on the Town Hall's doorstep, a local carpenter restoring dozens of the original heritage tables and chairs.

Thanks to the Trafford Local Studies team I had access to a wealth of documentation about the building of the Town Hall in the 1930s – invoices, letters, blueprints – and in the subsequent book was able to contrast the then and now.

The final result – a beautifully-restored heritage building and a two-storey extension with the highest sustainability credentials – was indeed a transformation.

"One summer it was unbearable. I think it got up to 33 degrees. You'd get hot and sweaty and sticky and were forever getting up to go for a walk to cool down. Because we can't open any windows it can get extremely stuffy.

"The winter would be just as bad. You'd sit here in coats, hats, scarves, gloves, the lot. You can't type wearing gloves. If you look around you can see we've all brought our own heaters from home. And there are fans everywhere. We've all got a heater and we've all got a fan... and we have to use them."

Trafford Town Hall 2011-13

Commissioned by the Shepherd Group and 5plus architects

Published as All That is Good by 5plus architects, 2013

23rd May 2011: 'First trip to Trafford Town Hall. Like stepping back in time to the 1970s. Archaic. How does anything get done? Lots of unhappy-looking people. Lots of potential for 'before' pictures but what about the structure of the project? Should it be narrated? By a previous mayor; the construction manager; a staff member?'

'.... the 1983 extension is not of interest.'
English Heritage list entry number: 1391923.

"You can curve it, you can bend it, you can stretch it, you can shape it. Lead is the best material in the world to work with."

"When they built the extension they took out sections of stone from the old Town Hall and, luckily for us, kept it on site; we're now cutting it up to use for repairs."

Archive records show the construction of the original Town Hall was administrated for the Council almost exclusively by one man. GH Abrahams, clerk to Stretford Urban District Council, corresponded with architects Bradshaw Gass and Hope on every sub-contractor appointment, every estimate considered and every contract issued.

The main contractor was Messrs E. Marshall and Sons Ltd, an all-round joiners, builders, contractors and timber merchants from nearby Ashton-under-Lyne. Their letterhead boasted, '...all kinds of repairs attended to promptly by practical men.'

Once suppliers had completed their contracts, Bradshaw Gass and Hope provided them with 'architects' certificates' which they presented to Abrahams with their invoices. On Abrahams' recommendation, the building sub-committee subsequently authorised payment. Mr Bertram Thomas of Hulme was paid £575 for 'electrical lighting, power, safety lighting, door bell and call bell installation'. The Synchronome Co. Ltd. of London charged £120 for installing electric clocks; a 'blowpipe and drill resisting safe' was supplied for £180 by Chubb and Sons of Albert Square, Manchester; and Asbestos Cement Building Products charged £67 7s 6d for installing asbestos pipes between the heating boiler and the flue.

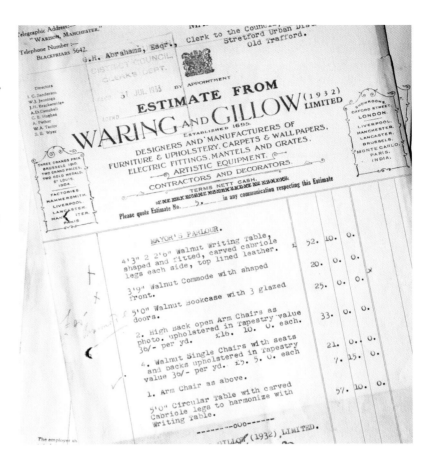

"... This building is our heritage and our past, but also our future. In short, this is a building for the 21st century and fit for a 21st century council. And, I have to say, it's good to come home!"

Councillor Matthew Colledge
Leader of the Council
24th April 2013

"... and may those who engage in the administration of the borough's affairs have only one object in view: The good government and welfare and happiness of its citizens..."

Earl of Derby
16th September 1933

Trafford Town Hall

"My favourite bit? I think it has to be the 'street'.
I absolutely adore it. When I have two minutes
I just stand in different places and watch how the
light floods into the buildng."

The transformation of
Trafford Town Hall won
the North West Regional
Award and the North
West Sustainable Building
of the Year Award from the
RIBA in 2014.

Trafford Town Hall

At school I gave up Art for Biology. I was marginally more interested in dissecting frogs than drawing a still life of upturned chairs. Throughout my adult life I have occasionally attempted to draw but with little success.

In January 2013, I visited Streetview, an exhibition in Manchester's Northern Quarter curated by city-loving blogger, researcher and guide Hayley Flynn, aka Skyliner. The show included work by some big-hitting local artists and designers but it was the loose sketches of the recent demolition of the BBC studios by illustration student Michael Morrell that inspired me.

That exhibition coincided with my friend Simone Ridyard, architect and educator, setting up the Manchester 'chapter' of Urban Sketchers, a worldwide movement of creative types who like to 'see the world, one drawing at a time'.

Almost by accident I had discovered sketching. At first it became an all-consuming hobby until, in 2015, I plucked up the courage to offer it as an alternative to my photography.

Since then it's become a perfect addition to my storytelling reportoire.

Cathedral Gardens,
January 2014

31st May 2014: 'I'm about to enter my 25th year as a photographer. I'm also at a turning point. I have some new projects and I'm in need of inspiration for them. I'm tired of doing them the same way.

'Paul Arden [*It's Not How Good You Are, It's How Good You Want To Be*], talks of the life-cycle of creativity. 50 is apparently the watershed. Before that you are repeating yourself. After that you reinvent yourself. I feel like I am repeating myself, particularly over the construction jobs. So, do things differently...'

Right: Manchester International
Festival, Albert Square, July 2015

"FIFTEEN YEARS AGO THEY SAID THERE'D BE RICH PEOPLE AND POOR PEOPLE LIVING SIDE BY SIDE. IT'D BE LIKE SALT AND PEPPER THEY SAID.

"BUT WE DON'T MIX. WE RARELY SEE OUR NEIGHBOURS ON THAT SIDE. NOBODY STOPS FOR A CONVERSATION."

LILLIAN

We need to get all these weeds out.

CATHERINE GETS SOME HELP WEEDING THE RAISED BEDS

CALLUM IS ONLY THREE...

EEK! Get that wiggly worm away from me, Callum!

STEVE'S HERE WITH THE COMPOST

Would you like to plant some butternut squash, Catherine? Have you seen them in Aldi? Big, they are.

I use my tablet to request repeat prescriptions online. It's so easy.

For my first sketching commission in 2015 (top) I became reacquainted with some Ancoats residents for a project aimed at re-energising community spirit.

Since then I've told stories for housing associations, councils, charities, universities and the NHS.

Sown in Bolton, 2016 (above), tells of an estate-wide food growing initiative, and (right) my sketches and interviews provide the creative content for a Manchester City Council digital inclusion campaign, 2019-20.

I went to school in Rusholme and now negotiate its cycle path several times a week. And, as the familiar is often invisible to us, it didn't immediately present itself as a subject for my first long-term sketching project.

With its plethora of curry houses, fashion stores, barbers, jewellers and takeaways, it soon became the venue for my weekend sketching.

Drawing in a shisha bar or on my tiny stool outside a greengrocers, I'd be sure to strike up a conversation with a shop owner or passer-by.

I'd post these encounters almost weekly on the blog before compiling my 96-page book that celebrates a unique neighbourhood in our diverse city.

PROJECT:

**The Rusholme
Sketcher
2017-18**

First a year-long blog (www.
therusholmesketcher.co.uk)
and then published in 2018
by Len Grant Books

As I'm finishing off the watercolour three men come in, one of them clearly very excited.

"We've just driven from London. This is our first stop in Manchester," he says. "We haven't even been to our hotel yet. My mouth is literally watering. I'm craving this food."

"What have you ordered?" I ask.

"The classic kobeda kebab. Which is what this place is known for and has been for years. I went to medical school here in Manchester. I used to live round the corner. You can read the ratings on Tripadvisor, five star is too low for this place."

"And you can't find anything like this in London?"

"To be honest with you," he says, handing over his cash, "I can't find anything like this in the world."

"One minute one shop closes and the next minute another opens. It's like life, always changing."

Ibrahim, Rusholme window cleaner

By way of explanation I pass one of my postcards to the two men closest to me. "Do you mind if you're in my drawing?" I ask.

The second looks from the postcard back up to me: "I follow you on Instagram!" says Hazaifa, "are you the actual bloke, the Rusholme Sketcher?" I sense some disappointment.

It's Portugal versus Iran, plus it's over 24 degrees, so the shisha bars are crammed. Every chair and shisha pipe is called into service.

I'm unsure of the crowd's allegiances until Portugal score just before half time. Quaresma's goal seems to divide the fans into two equal camps. The waiters could always double up as stewards.

Mayfield, a 24-acre site just south of Piccadilly Station, includes a derelict former railway station and a neglected river, and is the city's next big regeneration story.

Once complete it'll be a mix of office, retail, leisure and residential. In the meantime the Mayfield Partnership – a joint venture between LCR, Manchester City Council, Transport for Greater Manchester and regeneration specialist, U+I – has found imaginative ways of using the spaces, from hosting Manchester International Festival and The Warehouse Project in its cavernous undercroft, to renting out redundant workshops to start-up businesses.

For me, Mayfield Stories is a natural extension to my photographic storytelling. Documenting the beginnings of yet another chapter in Manchester's revival is as much a privilege as following the construction of The Bridgewater Hall or Manchester Arena was nearly three decades before.

Mayfield will have a new park as its centrepiece, the first in the city centre for a century. In Mayfield Sketchbook 1, I followed the consultation process as the design team listened to local people, schoolchildren and professional peers about their aspiration for a new, much-needed open space.

COMMISSION:

Mayfield Stories
2019 -

Commissioned by
The Mayfield Partnership

Produced as a series of 104-page sketchbooks

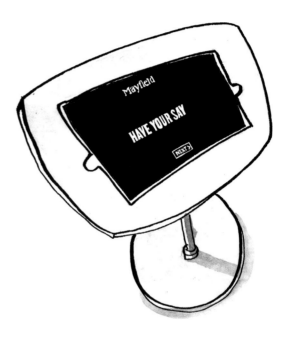

"These buildings have soul, they have heritage... and that's what people connect with."

James Heather, development director, U+I

The derelict entrance to the Mayfield Station platforms

Sketchbook 1 featured the pop-up food and drink stalls in the outdoor courtyard

Frank's first job with the Post Office was as a postman in Denton before he worked the parcels...

"You could earn so much money from overtime [at the Mayfield parcel depot] they used to call it the Golden Nugget.

"The main parcel office was further up Travis Street and that's where we'd do our regular shifts. Once you'd done your eight hours there you'd walk down the road and do overtime at Mayfield Station unloading the trains.

"When we got really busy and the sorting office couldn't cope, we'd take the bags down below in the undercroft and do a rough sorting there. We'd call it the rat hole. It was such a depressing place, like a prison."

Contemporary designers, Easy Peel, make good use of Mayfield's temporary space:

"It's difficult to pigeon-hole us," says Vinny. "We design and make things – furniture is a big part of it – but we also focus on public engagement, workshops and interactive design."

"Ultimately what we do changes from week to week," says Tom, "but our approach remains the same."

Dan Makin and his team have brought 2,000 tonnes of clean clay into an empty warehouse to create Dirt Factory, an indoor bike park. "It's a very different way of working. They've got all these assets around them which are eventually going to be demolished so it's a no-brainer to put them to good use," he says in in Mayfield Stories Sketchbook 2. "It brings people here and gets people talking about the place. And hopefully, as we've found, the community benefits in the meantime."

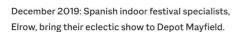

December 2019: Spanish indoor festival specialists, Elrow, bring their eclectic show to Depot Mayfield.

With the signing of a new lease the future of the Star and Garter pub – Manchester's iconic indie live music venue – has been secured. For Sketchbook 2, I chatted to Ian, the pub's long-standing maintenance man, doorman and one-time barman.

"We've had Status Quo, The Courteeners, Half Man Half Biscuit, Frank Crater and the Rattlesnakes, loads. I went to a UK Subs gig – as a paying customer – and thoroughly enjoyed the performance of those ageing but energetic rockers.

"The Smiths Discos and Smile nights are legendary."

Mayfield Stories

Books

PAGE 28

Arena!

Published by Len Grant Photography, 1995
My first photobook, charting the construction of
Manchester Arena, 1992-95
Edited by Anna Fox, introduction by Deyan Sudjic
ISBN: 0 9526720 0 6; 96 pages; 240 x 270mm, softback
Designed by Hemisphere Design

PAGE 36

Built to Music, The Making of
The Bridgewater Hall

Published by Manchester City Council, 1996
Commentary by Philip Thomas
ISBN: 1 872650 02 3; 96 pages, 315 x 245mm, hardback
Designed by Hemisphere Design

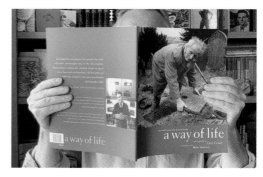

A Way of Life: Portraits
from the Funeral Trade

Published by Len Grant Photography, 1999
Introduction by Blake Morrison
ISBN: 0 9526720 1 4; 48 pages; 300 x 245mm, softback
Designed by Hemisphere Design

In 1999, in sharp contrast to photographing
regeneration, I completed a personal project –
portraits and interviews – about those working in
the funeral industry. The work was produced as a
touring exhibition (Viewpoint Gallery, Salford and
MAC, Birmingham) and a 48-page book.

'Len Grant has investigated the people who work
with death, and brought them to life. The shadowy
figures, unseen workers, and essential rituals are
given voices, faces, and environments. All this
achieved with time, integrity and some considerable
photographic skill.'

Zelda Cheatle, Zelda Cheatle Gallery, London

PAGE 62

Making the Lowry

Published by Lowry Press, 2000
Written by Jeremy Myerson
ISBN: 1 902970 04 7; 176 pages; 280 x 235mm, hardback
Designed by Hemisphere Design

The Mancunian Way

Published by Clinamen Press, 2002
Commissioned by Manchester City Council and published
to coincide with the Commonwealth Games 2002. With
photographers Jan Chlebik and Paul Herrmann. Edited by
Jane Price
ISBN: 1 903083 81 8; 160 pages; 290 x 220mm; hardback
Designed by Axis Graphic Design

PAGE 97

Making Manchester 1990-2003

Published by Len Grant Photography, 2003
To accompany my mid-term retrospective exhibition at
Cube, Manchester
Essays by Phil Griffin and Sue Vanden
ISBN: 0 9526720 2 2; 96 pages; 160 x 160mm; softback

Designed by Hemisphere Design

Space to Inspire

Published by Groundwork North West, 2004
A profile of Groundwork's community environment
programme in east Manchester
ISBN: 0 9547102 0 7; 64 pages; 195 x 155mm; softback
Designed by Hemisphere Design. This book won a Roses
Design Award 2003 for Best Use of Photography

PAGE 98

Cardroom Voices

The first of two New Islington books
Published by Len Grant Photography, 2004
ISBN: 0 9547281 0 6; 48 pages; 220 x 220mm; softback
Designed by Via

PAGE 114

Full Time at Maine Road

Published by Len Grant Photography, 2004
Includes an introductory interview with Radio 2's
Mark Radcliffe
ISBN: 0 9526 7203 0; 128 pages; 240 x 200mm; softback
Designed by Axis Graphic Design

A Portrait of Manchester

Published by Halsgrove, 2004
A Manchester 'coffee table' book
ISBN: 1 84114 380 4; 144 pages; 210 x 225mm; hardback

The Reluctant Engineer and other Manchester stories

Published by Martin Stockley Associates, 2006
ISBN: 0 9552408 0 8; 80 pages;
230 x 165mm; hardback
Designed by Axis Graphic Design

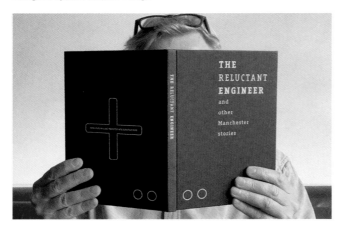

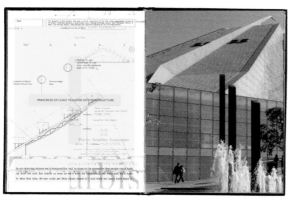

This alternative monograph tells of civic engineer Martin Stockley's contribution to Manchester's regeneration since his arrival in the city in 1993.

At first he was the 'northern envoy' for his London firm of engineers but later moved north and set up his own practice. He then collaborated on a masterplan for the Great Northern Warehouse/ G-Mex area of town and, while working on improvements to our canal infrastructure, began a long association with Piccadilly Basin. By 1996 he was well placed to join the local design team – with Ian Simpson and Nick Johnson – that helped draw up the post-bomb city centre masterplan.

Of the masterplan he noted: 'There were three things that we were absolutely clear about from day one. First of all we knew that Shambles Square had to go. There was no way we were going to get through to the Cathedral, and to Chetham's, and to that big car park that became Urbis and Cathedral Gardens, if we didn't get rid of Shambles Square.

'Secondly, we knew that the Arndale had to stay. There was never any question of it being demolished. It's a brute of a building and the bomb only knocked a few finishes off. But it had to stop being a rude neighbour and turn to face the street and put shops at street level.

'The third key thing was getting the quality of the public realm right. This was the busiest part of the city with all its shoppers and office workers but the pavements were atrocious. They just weren't wide enough. So it was essential we grasp this opportunity to make some radical change.'

Martin's Manchester regeneration experiences mirrored my own – we both also worked in Ancoats, on New Islington and, once this book was published, on Carver's Warehouse (see p.134). It seemed logical to Martin that I help him compile his personal Manchester history.

We worked with designer Alan Ward and, with my photographs, Martin's sketches, diagrams and plans, we produced a 80-page hardback book that gives an intriguing insight into an engineer's input to some of the city's major developments.

PAGE 108

Our House

Published by Len Grant Photography, 2006
To accompany the Lowry exhibition of the same name
Essay by Phil Griffin
ISBN: 978 0 9526720 4 3; 160 pages;
220 x 150mm; softback
Designed by Victoria Spofforth and Alan Ward
at Axis Graphic Design

From The Ground Up,
New Islington 2001-2007

Published by Len Grant Photography, 2007
The second of my New Islington books.
ISBN: 978 0 9526720 5 0; 120 pages;
220 x 220mm; softback
Designed by Via

'I think the book is a triumph. I found myself
celebrating the human condition as well as
despairing at the circumstances of some of the
individuals. It provides an essential counter balance
to the drive for output numbers and reminds us
that it is homes and lives we are dealing with rather
than bricks and mortar. It is now prescribed reading
in my office.'

Mark

PAGE 98

Carver's Warehouse

Produced for Town Centre Securities, 2008
Afterword by Martin Stockley
72 pages; 335 x 240mm; hardback, with slipcase
Designed by Axis Graphic Design

PAGE 134

PAGE 122

Reclaiming East Manchester

Published by Len Grant Photography, 2010
ISBN: 978 0 9526720 6 7; 184 pages;
240 x 160mm; hardback
Designed by Axis Graphic Design

PAGE 139

Billy and Rolonde

Published by Len Grant Photography, 2010
ISBN: 978 0 9526720 7 4; 128 pages;
250 x 190mm, hardback
Designed by Axis Graphic Design

100 Years in the Making

Produced for Cargill, Manchester, 2011
Another collaboration with designer Alan Ward, this 128-
page book was prepared for Cargill – a glucose factory on
the banks of the Manchester Ship Canal – as part of their
centenary celebrations.
240 x 170mm; softback with dustjacket and slipcase

Shooting the Breeze

Produced by Len Grant, 2011
A collaboration with poet Linda Chase
Additional photography by Mario Popham
86 pages; 180 x 180mm; softback
Designed by Axis Graphic Design

Linda and I set up our makeshift studio – from
an unwanted curtain – in four corners of the city,
and invited passers-by to be photographed and
interviewed. The subsequent poems and images
came together as a one-off performance and
small book.

The Reclaim Book

Published by Len Grant Photography, 2011
Foreword by Eric Allison, prison correspondent,
The Guardian
ISBN: 978 0 9526720 8 1; 136 pages;
230 x 170mm; softback
Designed by Axis Graphic Design

In The Reclaim Book I tell the story of an
inspirational Manchester charity that supports
young people from low income backgrounds.

A thoroughly enjoyable commission from which
I learnt a lot, not just from the selfless staff,
but from the teenagers I photographed and
interviewed. I met Frances, the subject of Her First
Year (p.142), at Reclaim.

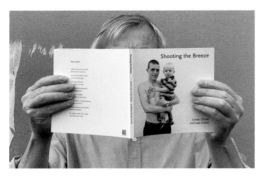

"Working with Len on this book has been a brilliant
experience for all of us... we are utterly delighted
with the finished book. It is witty, personal, poignant,
detailed, beautifully photographed and designed but
most importantly, it reflects the truth of our work."

Ruth Ibegbuna, Director, Reclaim

'Shooting the Breeze sums up everyday street life in
Manchester in a way that no one else has tried to do.
It tells the biggest story of an ordinary city through
the small stories of its ordinary inhabitants – and
makes fascinating reading.'

Dan Feeney, *Creative Tourist*, 2011

'I Grew That': Nurturing Strong Communities

Produced for Forever Manchester, 2013
An alternative evaluation of The Fair Share Trust
112 pages; 230 x 170mm; softback
Designed by Axis Graphic Design

PAGE 146

1 Angel Square

Published by Manchester University Press, 2013
Foreword by Sir Howard Bernstein
ISBN: 978 0 7190 9110 0; 260 x 210mm; 160 pages;
hardback
Designed by Axis Graphic Design

PAGE 154

All That is Good,
The Redevelopment of
Trafford Town Hall

Produced for the Shepherd Group and 5plus architects,
2014
225 x 225mm; 168 pages; hardback
Designed by 5plus architects

Rock Bottom, the first year of Jobs,
Friends and Houses

Produced for Jobs, Friends and Houses CIC, 2016
Set up by a Blackpool police sergeant, this innovative
rehabilitation programme saw addicts train to renovate
properties in the coastal town.
230 x 170mm; 160 pages; softback
Designed by Axis Graphic Design

PAGE 162

The Rusholme Sketcher

Published by Len Grant Books, 2018
ISBN: 978 1 9164873 0 7 148 x 210mm; 96 pages, hardback

PAGE 164

Mayfield Stories Sketchbook 1

Produced for the Mayfield Partnership, 2019
The first in a series of sketchbooks charting the
development of Mayfield, Manchester
175 x 125mm; 104 pages, softback
Designed by Axis Graphic Design

Parking a Poem in a Biscuit Factory

Published by Creative Scene, 2020
Written, photographed and illustrated by me, this book
examines the 'cultural ecology' of West Yorkshire.
Introduction by Jonathan Gross and Nick Watson;
Afterword by Nancy Barrett
ISBN: 978 1 9162816 0 8; 112 pages; 220 x 170mm; softback
Designed by Axis Graphic Design

Regeneration Manchester
30 years of storytelling

Published by Manchester University Press, 2020
ISBN: 978 1 52615798 0 ; 290 x 210mm; 178 pages; hardback
Designed by Axis Graphic Design

Regeneration Manchester has been kindly supported by

Buttress   **u+i**   **urbansplash**

Many thanks to the crowdfunding backers who have enabled this book to be printed

Haseeb Ahmed

Àgata Alcañiz

The Almonds

Nick Amatt

Nick Andrews

Tracey Annette

Art with Heart

David Ashton

Lisa Ashurst

Andy Avery

Axis Graphic Design Ltd

Sean Baggaley

Yvonne Grimshaw Baker

Richard Ballam

Lyn Barbour

Pamela Barnes

Nancy Barrett

Phil Barton

Carol Bartram

Tom Basford

Liesl Beckles

Patricia Beddow

Simon Bedford

Steve Bennett

Emma Bennett

Adrian Bentley

Don Berry

Kevin Bigham

Fiona Bleloch & Kevin Shryane

Nick & Fi Borland

Kieran Brennan

Andrew Brooks

Maria Brunelli

Simon Buckley

Kathryn Bullen

Paul Burns

Michael Burrows

Debbie Burton

Sarah Butler & Matthew Boardman

Roger Bygott

Anne Byron-Hehir

Adrian Calvert

Isabel Carmona

Sarah Carne

Ben Cavanagh

Lesley Chalmers

Marc Chapman

Oliver Childs

Kai Chisnell

Jan Chlebik

Anne Clayson

Philip Clegg

Robert Cohen

Steve Cole

Ryan Conlan

Nigel Corrigan

Tony Cottam

Stephen Coulthard

James Creegan

Mark Crossfield

Glenn Cunningham

Tessa Dadley

Mary & Paul Daly

Suzanne Dawson

Janice Dent

Neil Doyle

Sally Duncan

John Dwan

Ben East

David Eaton

Christophe Egret

Carol & Mariano Elices

Angela El Kholy

Martin Ellerby

Leon Ellis

Victoria Empson

David & Rona Epstein

Lyn Fenton

Susan Ferguson

Duncan Firth

Catherine Flannery

Patrick J Fogarty

Jim Forrester

Ric Frankland

Sarah Franklin

Matthew Frost

Sabrina Fuller

Helen Fuller

Beatrice Gelsi

Lawrence George Giles

Jonathan Gimblett

Stephen Gleave

Berrin Golding

Rebecca Goulding

Gill Gourlay

Libby Graham

Helen Grant

Jacky Grant

Sally Grant & David Buckingham

Simon & Anita Grant

Pat Gray

Ben Greenaway

Claire Griffiths

Paul Grivell

Reinhard Guss

Gareth Hacking

Maria Hallows

Vanessa Hamnett

Elizabeth Harding

Louise Hargan

Jo Hart

Peter Haymes

Paula Helsby

Noel Hennessy

Anna Henshall

Paul Herrmann

Alec Herron

Nicholas Higham

Sara & Marcus Hilton

Rachel Hirst

Brian Hodgkinson, in memory of William Hodgkinson

Marie Hodgson

Vicky Holliday

Kate Holmes

Eve Holt

Paula Hope

Daniel Hopkinson

Nick Hopkinson MBE DL

Lesley Hopwood-Ryan

Rebecca Horrocks

Megan Houghton

Roz Hughes

B Hunter

Peter Hunter OBE

Daniel Idama

In-Situ

Linda Isted

Ruairidh Jackson

Charles Jarvis

Adam Jefford

Karen Jones

Archie Jones & Victoria Ribbons

Janine Kellett

Chris Kelly

David Kerford

Ian & Lisa Kershaw

Ciara Leeming

Richard & Elaine Lees

Gideon Leventhall-Airley

Mark Lewis

Martin Livesey

Ruth Livingstone

Jason Lock

Simon Long

Jimmy Lu

John Lynch

Kathy McArdle

John & Nancy McAuliffe

Lucy McCarthy

Scott McCrory

Sean McGonigle

Will McHugh

Georgia McMahon

Paul McMahon

Andy McNee

Shelagh McNerney

Helen McPherson

Sheena Mediratta & Ajay Patel

Andrea Melarkey

James Millar

Peter Mitchell

Dan Moloney

Caroline Monk

Poppy Morch

Emily Morris

Paul Morris

Roger & Jennifer Moyle

James Mulvany

Pamela & Bryan Murphy, in memory of their father, Paul

David Nigro

Aidan O'Rourke

Maurice O'Shea

David Oates

Graeme Ogden

Alex Ormandy

Josh Owens

Grenville Page

Helen Palmer

Julie Palmer

Marie & Carl Parker

Alan Parry-Davies

Rob Paton

Andrew Pattinson

Iain Peacock

Michael Percival

Jack Perryman

Thomas Pierpoint

Planit IE

Liz Poole

Kirsty & Andrew Pope

Phil Portus

Alison Powell

Stephen Price

Jane Price

James Quinn

Palma Martina Raviele

Sarah Rawlings

Simone Ridyard

Charlie Roadnight

Glen Rollings

Alison Ruck

Leanda Ryan

Alex Saint

Bethan Schelewa

Mick Scholefield

Alison Scott

Ludovica Serratrice

Chris Sharratt

Terry Sheldon & Carole Isis Sheldon

Mandie & Pete Shilton Godwin

Michael Simpson

Chris H. A. Smith

Eddie Smith

Lucy Smith

Paul Smith

Stephen Smith

Matt Snodin

Andrew Start

Leo Steele

Gabriel Sterne

Patricia Sterne

Martin Stockley

Niki Stockton

Bernard Stone

Paul Stonehouse

Toby Stretch

Gary Sullivan

Martin Sullivan

Alex Summers

Kristian Sutcliffe

Swasky

Megan Swift

Jonathan Swinton & Emma Anderson

Matthew Taylor & Andrew O'Donnell

Michael Taylor

Lindsay Thomas

Ian T. Tilton

David Topham

Thomas Townson

William Trimble

Ruth Turner

Marlow Upton

Tom Urwin

Camila Varo & Ian Thompson

Dave Varty

Jonathan Vickers

Kate Vokes

Steven Wainwright

Catherine Walker

Rick Walker

Stuart Wallis

Aidan Walpole

Andy Walsh

Bethan Ward & Alex Paterson

Derek & Anne Ward

Seb Ward

Jane Ware & Adam McMahon

Dawn Warriner

Sue Watts

Julian Webb

Sam Whyte

Brenda Wile

Eibhlin Williams

Chris Williams

Sarah Williamson

Martin Wind

Barney Woodham

Paul 'Malpa' Worsley

Marcus Wroe

Izzy Wylie

Angela Young

With special thanks to Phil Doyle & Paul Norbury at 5plus architects

A 30-year retrospective book sounds like an ending. Not a bit of it. The coronavirus lockdown has given me the opportunity to rifle through my archives and re-visit my negative files. For me, this is merely a semi-colon, rather than a full stop.

I've recorded a compelling period in Manchester's recent past, but change is constant and there are always stories to tell. In the last few years I've challenged myself to learn a new way of telling stories and sketching now has a firm place in my repertoire. I'm looking forward to documenting the changing face of my city with a sketchbook and pen for many years to come.

Over three decades I've amassed a huge archive of images, both analogue and digital, as well as prints, notebooks, newspaper cuttings, publications and miscellaneous ephemera about Manchester's regeneration. I'm pleased that my collection will soon be welcomed into the city's own archives and find a new home in the basement of Central Library. It's a fitting way of giving back to the city.

It seems appropriate in this volume to thank those who've been instrumental in my career, thus far. An impossible task, of course. But let me attempt to express my gratitude in a generic way, hopeful that everyone gets included.

To all the clients who've 'got me', understood what I can deliver and given me the freedom to try new approaches. An open brief is often the best. Thank you.

To all my creative collaborators: fellow photographers and artists; designers; writers; poets; dramaturges; printers; exhibition builders; and picture framers. It's only through supportive collaboration that we all thrive. Thank you.

To all those friends and supporters who've witnessed my creative endeavours, pitching up at every exhibition opening and book launch. Thank you.

My special appreciation to my family: to Abigail, for her unconditional support and encouragement; and to our children, Rebecca, Ben and Daniel. This book is, ultimately, for you.

len_grant   #regenmcr

Afterword and Acknowledgements

September 2018: Photographed in a Rusholme barber shop by David Oates.